Penn Greek Drama Series

Series Editors
David R. Slavitt
Palmer Bovie

The Penn Greek Drama Series presents fresh literary translations of the entire corpus of classical Greek drama: tragedies, comedies, and satyr plays. The only contemporary series of all the surviving work of Aeschylus, Sophocles, Euripides, Aristophanes, and Menander, this collection brings together men and women of literary distinction whose versions of the plays in contemporary English poetry can be acted on the stage or in the individual reader's theater of the mind.

The aim of the series is to make this cultural treasure accessible, restoring as faithfully as possible the original luster of the plays and offering in living verse a view of what talented contemporary poets have seen in their readings of these works so fundamental a part of Western civilization.

Sophocles, 1

Ajax, Women of Trachis,
Electra, Philoctetes

Edited by
David R. Slavitt *a n d* Palmer Bovie

PENN

University of Pennsylvania Press
Philadelphia

10 9 8 7 6 5 4 3 2 1

Published by
University of Pennsylvania Press
Philadelphia, Pennsylvania 19104-4011

Library of Congress Cataloging-in-Publication Data
Sophocles
    [Works. English. 1998]
    Sophocles / edited by David R. Slavitt and Palmer Bovie
        p.   cm. — (Penn Greek drama series)
    Contents: 1. Ajax / translated by Frederic Raphael and Kenneth McLeish.
Women of Trachis / translated by Brendan Galvin. Electra / translated by
Henry Taylor. Philoctetes / translated by Armand Schwerner.
        ISBN 0-8122-3445-6 (v. 1: cloth : alk. paper). —ISBN 0-8122-1653-9
    (v. 1: pbk : alk. paper)
    1. Sophocles—Translations into English.   2. Greek drama (Tragedy)—
Translations into English.   3. Mythology (Greek)—Drama.   I. Slavitt,
David R., 1935–   .   II. Bovie, Smith Palmer.   III. Title.   IV. Series.
PA4414.A2   1998
882'.01—DC21   98-9962
                                                                                          CIP

Contents

Introduction

Palmer Bovie

Classical Greek tragedy, which flourished in Athens during the fifth century B.C., grew out of country festivals originating a century earlier. Three different celebrations in honor of Dionysus, known as the rural Dionysia, occurred during the winter months. One of these, the Lenaea, was also observed at Athens in the sanctuary of Dionysus. In addition to song it offered ecstatic dances and comedy. Another, the Anthesteria, lasted for three days as a carnival time of revelry and wine drinking. It also included a remembrance of the dead and was believed to be connected with Orestes' mythical return to Athens purged of guilt for killing his mother Clytemnestra.

The rural Dionysia were communal holidays observed to honor Dionysus, the god of wine, of growth and fertility, and of lightning. Free-spirited processions to an altar of Dionysus were crowned by lyrical odes to the god sung by large choruses of men and boys chanting responsively under the direction of their leader. The ritual included the sacrifice of a goat at the god's altar, from which the term "tragedy," meaning goat-song, may derive. Gradually themes of a more serious nature gained ground over the joyful, exuberant addresses to the liberating god, legends of familiar heroes, and mythological tales of divine retribution. But the undercurrent of the driving Dionysiac spirit was seldom absent, even in the sophisticated artistry of the masterful tragic poets of the fifth century.

Initially the musical texts were antiphonal exchanges between the chorus and its leader. Thespis, who won the prize of a goat for tragedy at Athens in 534 B.C., is traditionally said to have been the first to appear as an actor, separate from the chorus, speaking a prologue and making set speeches, with his face variously disguised by a linen mask. A fourth festival, the City Dionysia or the Great Dionysia, was instituted by the ruler Peisistratus, also in 534, and nine years later Aeschylus was born. It seems that the major era of Greek tragic art was destined to begin.

The Great Dionysia, an annual occasion for dramatic competitions in tragedy and comedy, was held in honor of Dionysus Eleutheros. Its five-day celebration began with a procession in which the statue of Dionysus was carried to the nearby village of Eleutherai (the site of the Eleusinian Mysteries) and then back, in a parade by torchlight, to Athens and the precincts of Dionysus on the lower slopes of the Acropolis. In the processional ranks were city officials, young men of military age leading a bull, foreign residents of Athens wearing scarlet robes, and participants in the dramatic contests, including the producers (*choregoi*), a resplendent in colorful costumes. The ceremonies ended with the sacrificial slaughter of the bull and the installation of Dionysus' statue on his altar at the center of the orchestra.

For three days each of the poets chosen for the competition presented his work, three tragedies and one satyr play (a farcical comedy performed in the afternoon after an interval following the staging of tragedies). In the late afternoon comedies were offered. The other two days were marked by dithyrambic competitions, five boys' choruses on one day, five men's on the other. The dithyramb, earlier an excited dramatic dance, became in the Athenian phase a quieter performance, sung by a chorus of fifty and offering little movement.

The theater of Dionysus at Athens was an outdoor space on the southern slope of the Acropolis. A semicircular auditorium was created on the hillside from stone or marble slabs, or shaped from the natural rock with wooden seats added. Narrow stepways gave access to the seats, the front row of which could be fitted out with marble chairs for official or distinguished members of the audience. From sites visible today at Athens, Delphi, Epidaurus, and elsewhere, it is evident that the sloping amphitheater had excellent acoustic properties and that the voices of the actors and the chorus were readily heard.

The acting area began with an *orchestra*, a circular space some sixty feet in diameter where the chorus performed its dance movements, voiced its commentaries, and engaged in dialogue with the actors. In the center of the orchestra was an altar of Dionysus, and on it a statue of the god. Behind the orchestra several steps led to a stage platform in front of the *skene*, a wooden building with a central door and doors at each end and a flat roof. The actors could enter and exit through these doors or one of the sides, retiring to assume different masks and costumes for a change of role. They could also appear on the roof for special effects, as in Euripides' *Orestes* where at the end Orestes and Pylades appear, menacing Helen with death, before she is whisked away from them by Apollo. The skene's facade represented a palace or temple and could have an altar in front of it. Stage properties included the *eccyclema*, a wheeled platform that was rolled out from the central door or the side of the skene to display an interior setting or a tableau, as at the end of Aeschylus' *Agamemnon* where the murdered bodies of Agamemnon and Cassandra are proudly displayed by Clytemnestra.

Another piece of equipment occasionally brought into play was the *mechane*, a tall crane that could lift an actor or heavy objects (e.g., Medea in her chariot) high above the principals' heads. This device, also known as the *deus ex machina*, was favored by Euripides, who in the climactic scene of *Orestes* shows Apollo protecting Helen in the air high above Orestes and Pylades on the roof. Or a deity may appear above the stage to resolve a final conflict and bring the plot to a successful conclusion, as the figure of Athena does at the end of Euripides' *Iphigenia in Tauris*. Sections of background at each end of the stage could be revolved to indicate a change of scene. These *periaktoi*, triangular in shape, could be shown to the audience to indicate a change of place or, together with thunder and lightning machines, could announce the appearance of a god.

The actors wore masks that characterized their roles and could be changed offstage to allow one person to play several different parts in the same drama. In the earliest period tragedy was performed by only one actor in counterpoint with the chorus, as could be managed, for example, in Aeschylus' *Suppliants*. But Aeschylus himself introduced the role of a second actor, simultaneously present on the stage, Sophocles made use of a third, and he and Euripides probably a fourth. From such simple elements (the orchestra space for the chorus, the slightly raised stage and its scene front, the minimal cast of actors) was created the astonishingly powerful poetic drama of the fifth-century Athenian poets.

What we can read and see today is but a small fraction of the work produced by the three major poets and a host of fellow artists who presented plays in the dramatic competitions. Texts of tragedies of Aeschylus, Sophocles, and Euripides were copied and stored in public archives at Athens, along with Aristophanes' comedies. At some later point a selection was made of the surviving plays, seven by Aeschylus, seven by Sophocles, nine by Euripides, and ten others of his discovered by chance. In the late third and early second centuries B.C., this collection of thirty- three plays was conveyed to the great library of Alexandria, where scholarly commentaries, *scholia*, formed part of the canon, to be copied and transmitted to students and readers in the Greco-Roman cultural world.

Sophocles (496 – 406 B.C.) was born at Colonus and lived as one of Athens' most admired artists and respected public citizens during the era of the city's prosperity, cultural glory, imperial expansion, and disastrous struggle against Sparta in the Peloponnesian War. In 443 he was elected imperial treasurer; he was elected general at least twice, once as a colleague of Pericles and later serving with Nicias after the Sicilian expedition. Among his friends were the philosopher Archelaus and the artist Polygnotus, who painted a portrait of Sophocles in the Stoa holding a lyre. He was a priest of the healing deity Alcon and made his own house a temporary place of worship of Asclepius until his temple was ready. In recognition of this reverential tribute Sophocles was honored as a hero after his death and awarded the title *Dexion*. A few months before his death he appeared at the preliminary to the Great Dionysia with his chorus, dressed in black, in mourning for Euripides. Such a generous public gesture well illustrates the noble character of his long-lived creative spirit.

Sophoclean technique differs from Aeschylean. Sophocles increased the number of chorus members to fifteen, from Aeschylus' twelve. The role of the chorus was, however, less closely attached to the actor's predicament; instead, the choral odes stand out in their lustrous lyrics as complementary interludes expressing themes of confidence and exaltation on the brink of a grim development in the plot. Or, in colorful imagery they trace the contours of a landscape animate with natural beauty; or describe a corner of the world of myth that bears on a situation in the drama. Like the sayings of an Aeschylean chorus, Sophocles' stage group will proffer somber advice or deplore the sinister turn of events.

In structure and style Sophocles advances the pace and clarity of action far beyond Aeschylus' crushing pageants of power. By introducing the third actor he gains more play in the thrust and counterthrust of dialogue. Electra can involve her sister Chrysothemis in the plan to destroy Clytemnestra; and when Chrysothemis argues for the preferable course of compromise, Orestes come into play as the avenging agent. Antigone contends with her sister Ismene as well as Creon; the latter's son, Haemon, adds to the interlocking tensions by opposing his father's sentence against Antigone. In the *Oedipus at Colonus* five different figures vie for Oedipus' good will: Antigone and Ismene, their brother Polynices, Creon, and Theseus—but the dominant personality of the aged Oedipus prevails in scene after scene, strong-minded and endowed with the mysterious power to confer blessings on the land of Athens.

Abandoning the trilogy, Sophocles studied related themes in different lights: *King Oedipus* was produced some fifteen years after *Antigone*, presented in 441 B.C. when Sophocles was fifty- four; *Oedipus at Colonus* was first produced the year after his death at the age of ninety in 405 B.C. Among his voluminous output of some 123 tragedies, Sophocles' recurrent interest in the fascinating myth of the Theban dynasty displays a masterful treatment of this complex narrative. *King Oedipus* delineates the classical model of the tragic hero, an admirable figure who, because of some flaw in character, mistakes his aim (*hamartia*) and undergoes a reversal of situation (*peripeteia*) which causes his downfall in such a spectacular manner as to evoke the combined feelings of pity and fear in the minds of the spectators. These were the terms applied by Aristotle in his fourth-century critique, the *Poetics*. Aristotle considered Sophocles' art to be a perfection of form, and certainly his judgment applies to *King Oedipus*. As the hero moves forward step by step in his investigation of the identity of the person responsible for the calamitous situation of Thebes, he gains his first insight into the possibility of his own involvement, at the exact center of the drama, line 715. He here first experiences "a wandering of the mind" on being told that Laius was murdered at a place "where three roads meet." Oedipus remembers that he himself had killed a man at such a place. From this point on, every new message intended as a reassuring piece of information becomes, ironically, one more bit of damaging evidence in the case against Oedipus himself, the misguided perpetrator of an unspeakable crime. Far different from the proud "tyrant," the ruler who at the beginning of his inquiry defiantly withstood the warnings of Creon and Tiresias and the concerns of his wife, Jocasta, Oedipus, the abject victim of his own obstinate intellect, has discovered the truth. It reduces him to fathomless sorrow and the frenzied violence of self-mutilation. He gouges out the eyes that have looked into the heart of the matter.

In legend, as *Oedipus at Colonus* shows, the hero, although brought to a wretched state of existence, blind and bedraggled, dependent on Antigone's arm for guidance, is not destroyed by his innocent plunge into criminal behavior. He has, rather, become schooled by his phenomenal suffering and is ultimately purified; graced with an aura of sanctity, he has acquired a mysterious power, associated with the virtuous will of the Eumenides. He exerts this redeemed power in the form of a blessing on Athens and its civic ideals under the leadership of Theseus, and vanishes into eternal life as a spiritual force for good.

The stalwart contenders in *Antigone* experience no such redemption but meet their fate in grim reality. The double dénouement carries the three principals briskly forward to disaster. Antigone confronts Creon, maintaining in ferociously brilliant terms the superiority of religious principles to Creon's blasphemous edict that Polynices' body be left to rot exposed and unburied. When Antigone is found to have defied the ruler's sacrilegious order by performing symbolic burial rites for her brother, she is sentenced to death by starvation in a rock-walled cave. Creon is then confronted by his son Haemon, the heroine's intended husband: the young man, outraged by his father's cruelty and pride, vows never to see him again and rushes away to try and save Antigone from her fate. Creon's next antagonist is the blind seer Tiresias, who pronounces stern warnings against Creon's misguided punishment of the maiden for her piety. Creon angrily accuses the soothsayer of mercenary motives, of "propheteering" by foretelling the future fraudulently. He stands at the summit of his hubris, the arrogant pride that has led him implacably from one error in judgment to another. The chorus of citizens now intervenes with Creon, urging him to relent, and he suddenly sees the wisdom of refraining from violence. He goes to Antigone's cave to release her. She has already found release in death by hanging herself. Haemon lunges at his father but misses and falls on his own sword in desperation. The reversal of situation is increased by one more degree when Creon's wife, on hearing the news of their son's death, commits suicide. Creon can only survey the wreckage and lament the disregard of divine law and his impetuous violence. Now he knows the truth, but it is the truth realized too late.

Characters in other dramas evince a similar passionate excess that leads to a rueful knowledge of their own errors. Philoctetes is persuaded to reverse his position and return to the Trojan war, indispensable to the Greek victory. Ajax eludes protection and takes his own life, but attains a reputation for glory nonetheless:

> You loved him.
> He was honest and just,
> he was a perfect man. (1568–70)

Deianira's suicide results from an innocent mistake: her gift to Heracles of the poisoned cloak. She dies unredeemed, mourned by her son who had accused her of treachery. Sophocles has trained his unwavering gaze on human vulnerability.

Electra attains twofold intensity by its portrayal of grief and then intrigue. The first half of the action reviews Electra's compulsive threnody. It is not so much that mourning becomes Electra as it is that Electra becomes mourning: she apologizes to the chorus for her unending refrains:

> Dear women! I am ashamed to have you think
> my laments are too many, my grief too much;
> but since I cannot help it, please forgive me. (246–48)

But hers is no state for moderate or pious conduct:

> My outrageous life has taught me how
> to do outrageous things. (213–14)

Both main elements of the play's craftily fashioned plot emerge in the opening exchange between the heroine and the chorus of Mycenean women. Electra's vengeful anger builds, shared in collusion with her sister Chrysothemis and sharpened in bitter invective by her confrontation of Clytemnestra with its nearing indictment of her mother's guilt. Following the false report of Orestes' death, Electra clashes with Chrysothemis over her plan to take vengeance at all costs. The sisters have converged, only to diverge—a favored dynamic in Sophoclean dialogue. Electra's grief has faded in the heat of her passionate hatred. But when Orestes first appears, disguised as a Phocian and bearing an urn allegedly holding Orestes' ashes, the mourning mounts again to an ironic level. Electra addresses the urn in her brother's hands in plangent tones with a sweeping elegiac remembrance of their days together.

The recognition scene sets the stage for Orestes' revenge, prompted and planned by his sister's stratagem. She is no longer the sorrowful victim but the epitome of vengeful hatred, glorying in the long-awaited revenge. When Clytemnestra's death cry is heard from within the palace, Electra exults on stage, shouting "Strike her again!" She wishes Aegisthus were there . . . and soon enough he appears. Orestes has hidden inside, but Electra greets the hated husband winningly and craftily maneuvers him into the shrouded presence of the body he assumes to be that of Orestes. But it is Orestes alive who reveals himself and Aegisthus' murdered consort at the final moment before dispatching Aegisthus himself. As the king courageously faces his fate, Electra makes her last demand:

> . . . Kill him now, and throw his body out
> for creatures who know how to bury his kind,
> far out of sight. This is the only way
> to free me from the weight of ancient crimes. (1439–42)

The architecture of Sophocles' well-proportioned structure is complete.

Ajax

Translated by
Frederic Raphael
and Kenneth McLeish

Translators' Preface

In Homer's *Iliad*, Ajax (or Aias) the son of Telamon led the contingent from the island of Salamis that sailed with the rest of the Greeks against Troy. The fleet was under the overall command of Agamemnon and his brother Menelaus, whose wife, Helen, had been seduced by Paris, son of the Trojan king. Ajax was said to be a huge man, the archetypal warrior: hesitant of speech and unhesitating in action. He carried a famously impressive shield and, after he and Hector had fought a duel that Ajax supposedly won on points, he wielded a sword given to him, in noble tribute, by his opponent.

After Achilles was killed, Ajax was mortified not to be confirmed as the best of the Greek warriors by being allotted the champion's arms. Instead, Agamemnon and Menelaus awarded them to Odysseus, who had less muscle but more clout than his rival. Ajax' death soon followed. Sophocles was possibly not the first to embellish the story by recounting how the hero went mad with rage and wounded vanity and finally killed himself, but the great tragedian certainly rendered that version canonical.

In other variations of his myth, Ajax is blessed as a baby by Heracles, and Zeus sends an eagle (*Aietos* in Greek) to signify that he will be a strong man. He is not always held to have killed himself. Paris is sometimes said to have shot him with an arrow and, in another story, he is so invulnerable to routine weapons that the Trojans can kill him only by burying him alive and then suffocating him with clay. Yet another, apocryphal gloss maintains that he was, at one stage, a pirate and a cattle-rustler. This idea lends irony to the Sophoclean version of the story, in which the hero steals the flocks of his erstwhile companions in arms before torturing and slaughtering them under the insane illusion that they are the Greek generals who have slighted him. His story would thus repeat itself, first as juvenile delinquency and then as tragedy.

Ajax is almost certainly a masterpiece of Sophocles' maturity. It stood by itself, not as part of a trilogy, in a program of four plays produced at the annual Great Dionysia. To be inventive was part of the challenge with which the Attic drama festivals faced competing tragedians. Since heroic, often Homeric myth supplied the staple plots of the majority of plays, what interested the audience (and could determine the allocation of prizes) was how the writer of a particular play contrived to "make it new" within the context of known stories and situations. In *Ajax*, Sophocles turned the almost comic myth of a bad loser into a tragedy of disappointment, folly, and divine partiality.

It is not only the human characters in the drama who are seen in a fresh light. Although Athena saves the Greek generals from Ajax' murderous venom, there is something callous both in her teasing of him and in the frigid pleasure she takes in his pathetic plight. Her protégé Odysseus' belated yet eloquent pity for the man who wanted to torture and kill him speaks better for human magnanimity than Athena's harshness does for her implacable consistency. Sophocles, traditionally renowned for his piety, here has something in common with Euripides, though he does not go quite so far as the younger man in his ironic treatment of the Olympians.

Ajax is, on the face of it, a tragedy with conventional features. Its action takes place within a single day, and it concerns a hero with a single flaw— not so much pride as vanity—that leads him to ruin. However, it also contains unusual elements. If it observes the "unity" of time, it does not honor that of place: we move from Ajax' tent to a deserted part of the beach, where with bitter irony he chooses to commit suicide with the very sword given to him by his enemy. Again breaching traditional rectitudes, Sophocles has the disgraced hero fall on his sword in front of the audience, rather than die discreetly offstage and have his death reported by a messenger. There is a further "Euripidean" touch in the prominence given to Tecmessa, Ajax' mistress and the mother of his child, Eurysaces: the infant has been named after the hero's famous shield but will clearly be incapable of protecting his mother from her lonely fate.

Tecmessa is an enslaved noblewoman who has been allotted (like a captive sheep) to Ajax, although she now clearly loves him. The reversal of her fortune, and the courage with which she endures it, may be symptomatic of a growing uneasiness, among some Athenians at least, about the "justice" and cruelty of war. As things continued to go badly for Athens in her war with Sparta, anti-war sentiment grew and became almost obsessional in, for instance, Euripides' *Daughters of Troy*, where the stoicism of women, especially when they have small children, contrasts with the irresponsible conceits and self-regarding postures of the warrior class.

The main characters in *Ajax*, however, are male. They are brilliantly differentiated and articulated. The eminently sane Odysseus is, as we have seen, the favorite of Athena, by whose vigilance Ajax has been prevented from decapitating the Greek army. He is duly, and carefully, grateful for the goddess' tutelage, but his humanity gives him more supple responses than the Olympian's. At the same time, although he is the most intelligent of the mortal characters, his evident alarm at the prospect of having to confront the crazed Ajax is a comic touch. Sophocles here contrives a certain convergence between tragedy and comedy. It is not easy to imagine the grandiloquent Aeschylus encouraging his audience to laugh at a tragic character. He would have sought to amuse them only in the satyr play, which was traditionally appended to a trilogy. What we see in *Ajax* is a discreet measure of lampoonery bleeding into the tragic form itself.

When the swaggering Agamemnon and the bombastic Menelaus want to deny the dead hero a proper burial, Odysseus challenges their officious vindictiveness. With no prospect of any dividend, the worldly hero sides, in common humanity, with Teucer. Despite his martial steadfastness, Ajax' brave half-brother has become the butt of the army's outrage at Ajax' depredations. Teucer is a marginal figure for two reasons: being an archer, he is a somewhat inglorious form of warrior; he is also a bastard, fathered by Telamon on a noble slavewoman, just as Eurysaces was by Ajax.

Between them, Ajax and Teucer supply a memorable portrait of a figure who never appears on stage: their father Telamon, who was himself a triumphantly gallant soldier until age forced him to return to his fiefdom of Salamis. Almost incidentally, and without any pause in the onward drive of the tragic narrative, Sophocles delivers a very "modern" account of the psychological motives that drove Ajax to feel ashamed of anything but complete success. Telamon is depicted an unsmiling, demanding role model for whom nothing but winning can count as success. His sons have been driven to emulate a man who refuses to be equaled.

Teucer's dread of his father is greater, we come to see, than that of the enemy he is always attacking. The death of his brother, which he could not have prevented since he was in the thick of battle, leads him instantly to guess that Telamon will accuse him of connivance and the hope of inheritance. The absent Telamon's bravery in war cannot conceal his heartless inadequacy as a father. Sophocles weaves into his drama an unforgettable image of an insatiably demanding father who resents his own loss of virility and cannot make way graciously for his heirs.

In the distinct characterizations of Agamemnon and Menelaus, Sophocles again reveals innovatory mastery. It would be tempting to argue that by bringing both generals onto the stage, one after the other, the playwright loses the opportunity for one climactic confrontation between the commander-in-chief and Teucer and Odysseus. What can be gained, a creative writing tutor might ask, by breaking the back of the last act? The answer is that Sophocles gives himself the opportunity to distinguish, entertainingly and with cumulative force, between the manifestly weak-strong Menelaus—the cuckold who always has to play the officious braggart—and the apparently strong-strong Agamemnon. Teucer deals very competently with the former; it needs the diplomatic nerve of Odysseus to face down the second. In addition to boldness, Sophocles adds a touch of "classical" symmetry: the brothers Ajax and Teucer are balanced by Agamemnon and Menelaus.

Ajax appears at first to be the story of an unintelligent lout who comes to lonely, sulky grief, but it is also a drama of reverberations and reactions. Its pace is subtly articulated. At the beginning, the apprehensions of disaster are artfully sustained by a sort of verbal slow motion: we overhear Ajax' conversation with Athena and then we hear an account of it, from another angle, from the uncomprehending Tecmessa. The unusually bloody, onstage depiction of Ajax' death avoids the need for a messenger scene and clears space and time for a more thorough dramatization of its consequences. Finally, there is an echo (or prefiguration) of the great moral debate of Sophocles' *Antigone*: whether the humane rite of respectful burial can ever be denied those who, in life, have offended powerful men or even the gods.

Odysseus, although in most regards a mere privileged spectator here, emerges as a worthy archetype of civilized "Western" man. With his astuteness and worldly wisdom, he combines urgent ambition with tactful awareness of the hazards of mortality and sympathy for the Other. Ajax is locked, and blocked, in his gigantic resentment; by his immutability, the great warrior is as doomed as the dinosaur. Odysseus may lack superhuman qualities, but his wit and resilience will allow his character to endure, in many forms, down the centuries.

TRANSLATORS' NOTE

Sophocles' Greek is full of exclamations—feoo, aee, oee moee, and so on. Each occurs in precise situations and seems to articulate a distinct emotional mood. Previous translations omitted them, or replaced them with anodyne English phrases like "alas" or "oh, woe." We have transliterated them but not interpreted them. We think that they may not have been intended to be spoken or sung exactly; rather, each gave the actor the cue for a vocal melisma or cadenza, spoken or sung: emotion distilled not into words but into pure sound. Research by Thanos Vovolis in the mid-1990s suggests that each sound may have resonated in the mask in a highly individual way. In workshops, actors have used the sounds in all kinds of ways, from inhalations of breath to improvised cries. Or they can be omitted: the choice is the performer's.

Cast

ATHENA, the goddess
ODYSSEUS, king of Ithaca, Greek warrior
AJAX, Greek warrior, son of Telamon and Eriboea
CHORUS of Ajax' sailors
TECMESSA, a captive princess, Ajax' concubine
SOLDIER
TEUCER, Ajax' brother
MENELAUS, king of Sparta, Greek warrior
AGAMEMNON, king of Mycenae, Greek warrior
NONSPEAKING
    Eurysaces, young son of Ajax and Tecmessa
    Attendants
    Soldiers

SCENE ONE

*(Outside Ajax' tent in the Greek camp outside Troy. Darkness before
dawn. Enter Odysseus. Athena speaks; at first he doesn't see her.)*

ATHENA

I'm always seeing you, Odysseus, on the prowl
for some enemy, on the lookout for some advantage.
And here you are again, where Ajax' sailors
pitch their tents. The back of beyond.
On the scent as usual, scanning the ground
for the big man's fresh-made footprints:
Is he in or is he out? If he's there, you'll find him.
You're like some Spartan hound, with your retriever's itch.
And he's there all right, your man's in there:
the lathered head all sweat, the killer hands   10
that swung the sword. No need to peek and pry.
First tell me what you think you're onto;
then hear the truth from one who knows.

ODYSSEUS

Athena speaks. Dearest of the gods to me.
I don't know where you are, can't see you,
but I hear your voice, it lifts my heart—
no war cry, no trumpet, ever sounds so clear.
You're onto me. I *am* sniffing round for Ajax,
Mister Fancy Shield. No friend of mine.
I'm on his trail; what other suspect is there?   20
Last night, he did something, *if* he did it,
that no one on earth would choose to see.
No one else could explain it; it fell to me,
as usual, to volunteer, to find out what happened.
We've just found all our cattle, our spoils from Troy,
slaughtered, their herdsmen hacked to pieces.
It's him. Where else to point the blame?
He was seen, skipping openly across the plain,
sword hot with blood. So we have a witness,
and now I want evidence. These tracks: 30
some are clearly his, the rest could be anyone's.
What should I do? Lady, thank God you're here.
As in the past, so now, my course is yours to guide.

ATHENA

I knew, Odysseus, and—such is my care for you—
I hurried here to help you.

ODYSSEUS

So then, dear lady: I've got it right?

ATHENA

He did it. He hurt you. The work is his.

ODYSSEUS

What madness made him do it?

ATHENA

Rage. They voted Achilles' arms to you, not him.

ODYSSEUS
Can that explain his coming down on *sheep*?   40

ATHENA
He wallowed in their blood and dreamt it yours.

ODYSSEUS
He thought he was killing *Greeks*?

ATHENA
Had I not been watching, he would have been.

ODYSSEUS
And thought he'd get away with it?

ATHENA
It was dark. He meant to pounce and run.

ODYSSEUS
And he nearly succeeded?

ATHENA
Agamemnon's tent, Menelaus' tent: as near as that.

ODYSSEUS
What stopped him? On the brink of murder: what?

ATHENA
I stopped him. Before his eyes
I conjured fantasies to thwart his glee,   50
turned his hand against cows and sheep,
Greek booty spoiled from Trojan farms,
guarded by yokels, unallocated still.
He fell on them, slashed their horny ranks,
like a scytheman in a meadow, cut a swathe of spines.
Now he was stabbing Agamemnon, Menelaus,
then another general, single-handed, and another.

I baited the trap; I rushed him into craziness.
When he was done, panting among the carcasses,
he roped the survivors and marched them home.   60
He thought them warriors; they were cows and sheep.
They're prisoners now, inside: he's torturing them.

I'll show you his madness, as clear as day:
I'll show you, you can tell the Greeks.
What's wrong? Are you afraid of him?
Don't worry: I'll baffle his eyes.
He'll see you, but he won't know who you are.

Inside. Stop racking those prisoners' limbs.
Come out. Yes, Ajax, you. I want you, now.

ODYSSEUS
What are you doing? Don't fetch him here.   70

ATHENA
Be quiet. What are you, afraid of him?

ODYSSEUS
In God's name, leave him where he is.

ATHENA
What can happen? He's just one man.

ODYSSEUS
My enemy. Today won't change him.

ATHENA
He's down, your enemy is down. Enjoy it.

ODYSSEUS
I'd rather he stayed indoors.

ATHENA
> He's mad—are you afraid to face him?

ODYSSEUS
> If he had his wits, I'd face him.

ATHENA
> He won't even see you.

ODYSSEUS
> He still has his eyes. 80

ATHENA
> I'll blur them.

ODYSSEUS
> As you wish. Gods do as they choose.

ATHENA
> Say nothing, then. Stand there.

ODYSSEUS
> I'll do it. Reluctantly, I'll do it.

ATHENA
> Ajax. Inside. It's me again,
> Your ally. Is this how you treat your friends?
> *(Enter Ajax. He carries instruments of torture.)*

AJAX
> Hullo, Athena. Daughter of Zeus, good morning.
> How glad I am you came. Gold necklaces for you,
> in thanks for the booty I've rustled up, inside.

ATHENA
> Thank you. But tell me: 90
> Your sword's well soused in blood, Greek blood?

AJAX

Oh, yes. I flatter myself it is.

ATHENA

Agamemnon, Menelaus: had a go at them?

AJAX

They won't be voting Ajax down again.

ATHENA

They're dead, the pair of them?

AJAX

Oh, now let's see them steal my arms.

ATHENA

And Laertes' son? Any luck?
Or did he get away?

AJAX

The fox of foxes, is that who you mean?

ATHENA

Your rival Odysseus, yes.   100

AJAX

The best tidbit of all, dear lady.
Got him sat in there. He won't die soon.

ATHENA

You're licking your lips. What plans for him?

AJAX

I'll tie him to the tentpole—

ATHENA

Ouch. Then what?

AJAX

Take a whip, make jam of him, and *then* he dies.

ATHENA

Add shame to all he's suffered?

AJAX

Lady, as a rule, your word, I jump.
But in *his* case, the sentence stands.

ATHENA

If that's your pleasure, enjoy yourself.   110
Don't flinch. Leave nothing out.

AJAX

I'm off to work. But hear the order of the day:
be always at my side and fight my fight.
(Exit.)

ATHENA

You see, Odysseus? What strength gods have?
Whose mind was clearer, once?
on the battlefield, who matched his skill?
Who knew better what to do or when to do it?

ODYSSEUS

I know of no one. No friend to me—
And yet I pity him, now he's undone,
and yoked like a beast to savage fate.   120
I see his fortune could be mine;
I see we're counterfeits, we mortals,
we're shadows, blown on the wind.

ATHENA

Remember that, say not one word
that puts you above the gods.
You're strong? You're rich?

Don't make too much of it.
A single day can sink a man
or raise him up: that's all.
When mortals show respect   130
we favor them; and if they don't, we don't.
(Exeunt. Music. Enter Chorus.)

CHORUS
Ajax, son of Telamon,
lord of sea-washed Salamis,
your success is ours.
But when the lash of Zeus
or slanders from Greeks torment you,
dread tenants our souls,
hearts pound, we're doves,
fluttering, wild-eyed.

Noise, rumors in the night: 140
scandal. Our lord's awake,
padding across the plains,
the fields of Troy, where cattle graze,
where sheep and cattle graze,
Greek spoils from Troy.
Knife gleams in the dark,
he stabs and stabs.

Scandal.
Odysseus whispers it,
drops poison in every ear.   150
Oh, they believe him, easy, easy,
they pass along your shame, and laugh to hear it.

Who slanders little men?
Only the great are envied,
heroes, princes,
our bastions in battle.

Even there, in the clatter and roar of war,
spite yaps at their heels.

But without their leader,
the rabble crumble.   160
We need each other:
We need our princes,
our princes need us,
can't survive without us.

Try teaching fools
to learn what they cannot.
That's why they shout against you now,
loudmouths shout;
our voices dare not answer them.
Speak up for us, lord,   170
look them in the eye,
shut their mouths,
make them tremble into silence,
as a hawk makes sparrows tremble.
Come out, dear lord, and speak.

Some god did this,
brought shame on us,
sent him springing against the cattle.
Was it Artemis, bull-Artemis,
daughter of Zeus on high   180
who mothered our shame?
Did he forget to honor her for victory,
hold back her battle-spoils, her hunting-spoils?
Or was it Ares, leaping in bronze,
our warlord, was it he we slighted?
Was this his punishment,
dark dealings in the night?

Some god did this,
stole Ajax' wits,

made him prance against cattle: 190
some god did this to you.
Apollo, Zeus,
it's done, so be it.
Still keep his reputation high.
Send him out, lord, out
from your tent beside the sea.
Answer them,
the whisperers,
their Majesties,
his Lordship of Ithaca: 200
they're stealing your name,
No. No. Come out
and face them down.

Lord, get up. Come out.
Don't rest from war too long.
You skulk inside,
hate blazes,
bonfires of hate
that sear the sky and scorch the winds.
Nothing stops them: 210
rumor, scandal,
tongues jangle.
They swagger,
they prance all over us:
our hearts are broken.
(The music changes as Tecmessa enters.)

TECMESSA
Friends,
Lord Ajax' friends,
his crewmen,
weep for him,
your prince so far from home,   220
weep for him.
Ajax is down,

our great one, our champion:
his pride is smashed,
his dazzle dimmed,
his strength storm-tossed.

CHORUS

Lady, what's happened?
Night treads on the heels of day:
bad news. Lady, dear lady,
our warlord's prize   230
beloved, chosen above all others,
what's happened? Tell us.
You're the one who knows.

TECMESSA

Find words: how can I?
It's worse than death:
he's mad, great Ajax,
in a single night
struck blind with madness.
Look, inside: his victims,
death-offerings, blood on his hands,   240
a hero and his fate.

CHORUS

Madness flares in him.
Unbearable. It's here.
It's time. It's inescapable.
His mind's on fire—
and the news is out,
their lordships know it,
it's ravenous, it grows.
Oee moee.
What will happen now?   250
If he killed those cattle,
their herdsmen in the dark,
if he lifted the blood-black blade, he's dead.

TECMESSA
  Oh moee.
  Prisoners-of-war he took from over there,
  a herd, a silly herd,
  he ripped them, gutted them.
  Two rams he took. White hoofs.
  Beheaded one, tore out its tongue,
  lashed the other to a tent-pole   260
  and flogged it, flogged it.
  His horsewhip whirred and whirred.
  He was cursing, shrieking,
  spitting his demons:
  a man possessed.

CHORUS
  We must hide.
  We must cover our heads and hide,
  or pull out to sea, row clear
  of the tide of their vengeance,
  Agamemnon, Menelaus.   270
  If we stand with him and face them,
  they'll stone us, stone us.
  His fate is sealed.

TECMESSA
  Be calm.
  He's calm. Storm over.
  Lightning ripped, winds howled;
  no more. He's sane again.
  His eyes are open. He sees what he did,
  what no one else has done.
  The pain of it, the bite: he knows.   280
(*Music ends.*)

CHORUS
  If it's over, things may yet be well,
  if the fit has passed. Less said, the better.

TECMESSA

    Suppose you had the choice—
    be happy by yourself,
    or, hand in hand, share the pain of those you love?

CHORUS

    Ours, theirs: pain doubled, pain twice as much.

TECMESSA

    He's cured. We're left with it.

CHORUS

    I don't understand.

TECMESSA

    When he was sick, he gloried in it,
    understood nothing: *we* knew his pain,   290
    felt shock and shame. And now he's sane,
    now he's come to himself, is free of it,
    resumes the horrors riding on his back—
    are *we* then free of it? Are we not the same?
    Heap pain on pain: is that a cure for it?

CHORUS

    You're right. Some god did this.
    He may be sane, but perhaps
    when he was mad he was happier.

TECMESSA

    If it's so, it must be so. Accept it.

CHORUS

    So he was . . . touched. How did it begin?   300
    Your grief is ours. So tell us.

TECMESSA

    What's mine is yours. You'll hear it all.
    It was pitch dark. The evening lamps

no longer flared. He reached for his sword—
that huge war-sword—and started out.
I didn't like it. "Ajax," I said,
"What are you doing? Why stand to arms?
Was there a trumpet? I heard no call.
The army's all asleep."
His answer? What men always say: 310
"A woman's best ornament is silence."

I've no idea, can't say, what happened next—
but back he came, with cattle roped like prisoners,
dogs, a flock of shaggy sheep.
He severed heads; turned others upside down,
slit and gutted them; tied others up
and racked them, you'd have thought them human.
Next minute he darted outside,
started boasting to some shadow there—
he was giggling—Agamemnon, Menelaus,   320
Odysseus: he'd paid them out, and how.
Then in he charged again. And all at once
he bent his head, slowly, painfully,
came to his senses, became himself again.
He saw the room all crammed with death,
and struck his head and yelped his shame.
Sat in the mud, there on that butcher's floor,
grabbed handfuls of his hair, sat still . . .

At first, no words.
Then he was shouting, shouting at me: 330
I was to tell him every detail,
what he'd done, what would happen now.
I was so afraid. I told him all I knew:
the whole disaster, all I knew of it.
He started sobbing like a woman,
sounds I'd never heard from him before—

only mommies' boys and babies ever wept like that,
he'd always said; you'd never hear
shrill keening from a warrior,
only bellowing, brave bellowing, bull-bellowing . . .   340

So now, flattened by Fate,
not eating, not drinking, our hero sits
numbed among bits of animals.
And there's worse to come:
to judge by his cries, his sobs,
there's worse to come.
Friends, *you* go in. Please.
I came to ask you. Do it.
You're his friends: he'll listen.

CHORUS
Tecmessa, daughter of Teleutas,   350
vile things you tell us of a man possessed.

AJAX *(off)*
Eeoh moee moee.

TECMESSA
Another fit. Did you hear?
Great Ajax, howling.

AJAX *(off)*
Eeoh moee moee.

CHORUS
Is he sick again? Or is it knowing now
what madness did that racks him so?

AJAX *(off)*
My son, my son.

TECMESSA

I can't bear this. He wants his son.
Eurysaces. What for? Where are you?   360
Please, what am I to do?

AJAX *(off)*

Teucer. Brother. Where are you?
Must you attack, attack, and I am lost?

CHORUS

Open the door. He sounds sane enough.
He'll see us; perhaps he'll be himself.

TECMESSA

I'll do it. See for yourselves
What he's done, what he's come to . . .
(Music. The doors are opened. Tableau: Ajax sitting among the
slaughtered animals. [Note: in the original Greek
production, Ajax' speeches as far as line 465, all in
lyric meters, were possibly sung or declaimed to
musical accompaniment, a standard practice in the
presentation of madness or extreme emotion; those
of Tecmessa and the Chorus, by contrast, were in
ordinary iambics, and were spoken.])

AJAX

Eeoh.
Friends, shipmates,
still loyal,   370
out of all the Greeks
who sailed to Troy,
only you still loyal:
see me, storm-tossed,
waves of blood,
I'm rolling, drowning.

CHORUS
  Tecmessa, what you told us was true.
  With our own eyes we see his madness.

AJAX
  Eeoh.
  Sailors, oarsmen,   380
  sun gleamed
  on your blades
  as they carved the sea,
  carved sea for Troy:
  help me, ease me,
  who else can help me?
  Butcher me, cut me,
  end me now, here, now.

CHORUS
  Don't ask it, lord. Pile pain on pain—
  in a sea of troubles, what help is that?   390

AJAX
  Look at me:
  high-hearted,
  my strong right arm,
  my courage ablaze in battle—
  and this is what I do, kill sheep,
  rage and triumph over sheep.
  Oh, look at me and laugh.

TECMESSA
  Ajax, no. Don't say this. Lord Ajax, no.

AJAX
  Don't touch me.
  Leave me. Go.   400
  Aee aee. Aee aee.
  Aee aee. Aee aee.

CHORUS
> In God's name listen, lord. Do as we tell you.

AJAX
> I'm lost.
> I had them in my hands,
> the wicked ones, who hurt me:
> I dropped them, I turned on sheep,
> on harmless sheep,
> sheep's thick black blood.

CHORUS
> It's over. Don't rack yourself.   410
> You'll never go back where you were before.

AJAX
> Eeoh.
> Laertes' son, Odysseus,
> fox of all evil,
> is he to see this now,
> see this and laugh?

CHORUS
> God's will, lord: laughter or tears, God's will.

AJAX
> I'd see to him,
> even now I'd see to him.
> Eeoh moee moee.   420

CHORUS
> No threats, lord: see where you are, be calm.

AJAX
> Zeus protector, father,
> he smiles, he lies,

all lies he is.
Let me tear him—and them,
those brothers, I spit on them,
those princes, let me kill them,
then kill me too.

TECMESSA

O Ajax, pray for me. If you must die,
pray for me, let *me* die too, die with you, die.   430

AJAX

Eeoh.
Light's turned dark
and day means night,
take me, snatch me,
open Hell's gates for me.
What god will pity me,
what mortal? Take me.
she hunts me,
Zeus' daughter,
pants after me   440
to ride me down—
no escape, no hiding.
What's left for me?
I'll lie with silly sheep,
till my army comes, my comrades come
and end me, end me.

TECMESSA

I'm done for.
that my lord should come to this,
my lovely lord. I'm done for.

AJAX

Eeoh.   450
Waves of the restless sea,

rocks, woods of Troy,
I smiled on you,
too long I stayed with you.
Death calls, must I leave you now?
Bear it, I must.
Scamander,
river of Troy,
little streams your children,
you smiled on Greeks,   460
now say goodbye,
never see me more.
Ajax the great,
no man in Troy, no Greek my equal,
here, humbled in the dust.

CHORUS
    Don't say such things. And yet,
    in the pit of misery, what else to say?
(Music ends.)

AJAX
    Aiee, Ajax! My name says what I feel:
    who'd have believed that pain and I'd be one?
    Aiee, Ajax! I say it twice,   470
    and then again, aiee, for what is happening.
    My father fought here at Troy,
    fought nobly, went home ablaze with fame,
    and I, his son, came here to this same place,
    to Troy, and matched him, strength for strength:
    this hand made no smaller mark than his.
    And now I'm done down, despised, by *Greeks*!
    Maybe, maybe: but one thing I think I know.
    Imagine Achilles alive, awarding the prize
    of his arms to the bravest of all the Greeks—   480
    who else would he choose but me?
    Instead, the sons of Atreus make the choice,

and that man, that nobody,
Mister Nothing, grabs the lot.
Away with Ajax!
Brave deeds win no prizes here.

My eyes were blind, my mind awry,
or I'd have fallen on them,
stopped them cheating any other man
the way they cheated me.   490
I'd have taken care of them.
But Athena, Her Ladyship, cold-eyed,
robbed my wits, made me falter,
pitched me into madness, fitted me up:
sheep's blood, not men's, now fouls these hands.
They've got away; *they're* laughing and laughing.
Is this my fault? When gods do you down,
be as strong as you like, your easy prey skips free.

What's left for me now? God hates me,
the Greeks, all Troy, the ground I stand on . . .   500
Go home? Sail the Aegean sea,
leave the sons of Atreus anchored where they are—
and show what kind of face to Telamon
my father? How could he look at me,
empty-handed, without a shred of glory,
when he was crowned with fame and greatness?
I can't, I won't. I could go to the city walls,
challenge the Trojans, one after another,
single combat, and die a gallant death.
To please the sons of Atreus?   510
I'm not having that. I have to find a way
to prove to my old father
that such as he could spawn no gutless son.
What warrior prolongs his life
when he's shamed, shamed beyond cure?
Is there a single day worth living

when life means no more than dodging death?
What prize can any man deserve
who lets illusion prime his hopes?
You live in glory or you die in it: 520
that's what the brave man does. That's it.

CHORUS

No fancy phrases here.
Ajax speaks as Ajax feels.
But now . . . do as we say. We're friends,
we care for you. Give way.

TECMESSA

Lord Ajax, we're mortal. Fate curses us,
evil of evils. Take me, for instance.
My father was a free man, a rich man, a prince
in Phrygia—and what am I now? A slave!
God willed it so, you'll say, but your hand did it.   530
I came to your bed; I cared for you,
and I beg you now, by Zeus who kindles hearths,
by the bed you share with me,
don't leave me to the jeers and jibes
your enemies will throw at me when I become
someone else's booty, someone else's prize.
When you die, I'm finished.
The Greeks will waste no time,
they'll pass me from hand to hand,
I'll be on my knees to them, begging,   540
your son at my breast. I'll grovel.
Who'll rub it in, who'll salt the wound?
"Look, Ajax' tart, who was the greatest man around!
Her Ladyship is on her knees!"
That's what they'll say. My pain, my lord,
your shame, yours and your family's!
Think of your father, dumped in sour old age;
your mother whose years bring her to this,
who prays and prays to see you home.

Have pity, lord! Your little boy,   550
how will he eat without you?
No friends, an orphan—will you do this to him,
to me? Oh think of me if you are gone,
you're all I have. Your spear ran through my world:
my mother and my father live with the Dead below.
Where can I turn, except to you?
how live, unless I live with you?
Am I not worth a thought? Remember me,
as men should remember, who pleasure knew.
Shouldn't love, now and then, breed love?   560
Coldness where kindness was,
answer smiles with frowns—
is that what rank and honor mean?

CHORUS
    Ajax, pity her, as we do.
    Our hearts weep tears for her.
    Accept what she says. Smile on her.

AJAX
    If I'm to smile,
    if she wants me to smile,
    let her earn it by doing as she's told.

TECMESSA
    How, sweet lord? Ask anything.   570

AJAX
    Bring *him* here, my son here, now.

TECMESSA
    I took him away . . . I was afraid . . .

AJAX
    When I was . . . is that what you mean?

TECMESSA

Afraid you'd hurt him if you saw him.

AJAX

In the state I was in, what else would I have done?

TECMESSA

I kept him away, kept him safe.

AJAX

You were right to do it.

TECMESSA

And now, dear lord, as things now are?

AJAX

Bring him here. I want him here.

TECMESSA

He's with the guards.   580

AJAX

Then fetch him. Now, at once.

TECMESSA *(calling off stage)*

Eurysaces, your father wants you.
You men, whichever of you has him, bring him.

AJAX

And quick about it. Are they deaf?

TECMESSA

They're coming. He's come. He's here.
(An attendant brings in the child Eurysaces.)

AJAX

Put him in my arms. Do it. He won't be afraid.
No son of mine will cry at a little blood,

at the sight of a little blood. He has to learn.
A hard school, his father's,
any trainer tells you that . . .   590
it's time for him to learn. Start young,

Son, be your father in everything, save luck:
be luckier. You'll be all right.
I wish I were you, right now,
seeing all of this, understanding none of it,
Innocence! Sorrow and joy:
they'll be yours one day, you'll grow up one day—
and when you do, son of Ajax,
show all your enemies whose child you are.
Till then, bask in the breeze, a sapling,   600
mother's darling, grow straight and strong.
The Greeks won't touch you. I won't be there,
but I guarantee respect:
Teucer my brother will watch you,
guide you, guard you. He's fighting now,
hunting Trojans, but soon as he returns,
unsleeping, unsparing, he'll devote himself to you.

You men, soldiers, who sailed with me
from Salamis, you're part of this.
I lay this charge on you all. Tell my brother,   610
tell Teucer my instructions: to take this child
to Telamon my father, Eriboea my mother.
He'll comfort them, support them,
till they tread Death's halls below.

As for my armor: it's not to be parceled out,
piecemeal among the army. Self-appointed judges,
and especially him, that man who ruined me—
they're to have no say. Look, child,
this is yours, this shield, seven bulls' hides thick,
its strap close-woven. Look here: your name,   620
Eurysaces. Touch it, hold it . . . it's yours.
The rest will be mine, all ready in my tomb.

Take him. Go inside. Shut the doors.
If you have to weep, weep there.
Women's tears, I won't have them here.
We're sick, we don't need wailing,
we need the knife. Go now. Go now.

CHORUS
Sharp words.
What do they mean?
I'm frightened.   630

TECMESSA
Ajax, lord, what are you so keen to do?

AJAX
Wait and see. Don't ask. Don't bother me.

TECMESSA
Oee moee. In God's name, lord,
for the sake of your son, don't abandon us.

AJAX
God's name, you say? Ridiculous!
I owe God nothing. My debts are paid.

TECMESSA
Lord, blasphemy.

AJAX
I'll hear no more of this.

TECMESSA
Please listen.

AJAX
I've heard enough.   640

TECMESSA
> Dear Majesty, I'm afraid. Afraid.

AJAX
> Go inside. And now.

TECMESSA
> In God's name, hear me.

AJAX
> Tecmessa, you're a fool. I won't.
> My time for lessons: done.
> *(Exit. Servants take away Eurysaces. Tecmessa remains. Music.)*

CHORUS
> Salamis,
> dear island,
> famous Salamis, beloved,
> mother of heroes,
> washed by the circling sea,   650
> lost to us now, forever lost.
> Here in these hills we lie,
> time dies for us,
> years die for us,
> hope dies, nothing's left for us
> but death, dark, emptiness.
>
> Look: Ajax,
> prince Ajax,
> a new grief now to bear.
> You mothered him,   660
> your champion. Oh moee,
> he's here, beached here, alone,
> locked in his mind,
> locked in madness,
> mocked by their Majesties,
> deserted, brave deeds forgotten.

In Salamis his mother,
whitened by the years,
counts out the past,
long days of the past.   670
She'll hear of this,
hear how he eats his own life.
She'll weep for him, weep for him,
no nightingale, soft tears,
but shrieks, sharp cries,
trembling hands beat breast,
tear thin gray hair.

To be trapped in madness,
vexed by vain fancies,
futile—why can't he die,   680
find peace in death,
our champion, noblest of Greeks,
Greeks born to sorrow, noblest?
He's lost, adrift, betrayed.
His father's waiting—who'll tell him
what's happened to his son?
He'll hear, he'll hear.
Alone of all Greeks,
this fate is his. Alone.
(Music ends. Enter Ajax.)

AJAX

Time defies our count. It's long,   690
and bears its fruit in darkness,
it buries what was bright.
All's possible. All changes.
One day, everything changes.
The solemn oath? Forget it.
The hardened heart grows soft.
Look at me. My mind made up,
like a tempered blade; then a woman pleads

and I soften, I pity her:
the helpless widow, my orphan child.   700

I'm going. The beach. The sea.
I must clean myself, wash foulness off.
The goddess rages; I must dodge her heat.

There's somewhere no one goes:
there I'll hide that sword of mine,
defiled and hateful, I'll dig a hole for it,
no one knows where. To Hell with it!
Black Night can keep it. Hector's it was,
he gave it me, that man who means Greeks no good.
And ever since they've despised me, shamed me.   710
The proverb's true:
An enemy's gifts, no gifts—they bring no joy.

I've learned my lesson: give way to God,
respect the sons of Atreus.
They're kings, we must bow to them.
All things in life, the strongest things,
the things we fear, accept authority, defer.
When sweet-fruited summer comes,
snowy winter steps aside;
when white-horsed Dawn rides out   720
to streak the sky, Night yields her weary watch.
Winds fret and moan, soothe grudging seas.
And Sleep himself, who takes us all,
first binds, then frees us: who sleeps forever?
One day we'll learn this lesson.
I've learned it already: hate your enemies,
but remember, one day they may turn friends.
And when it comes to friends, do all you can,
but don't expect to keep them:
friendship's anchored in loose and shifting sand.   730

That's enough. No more of it.
Woman, go in, pray God to grant,
in the fulness of time, my secret prayers.
(Exit Tecmessa.)
   And as for you, my men: obey, as she did.
When Teucer comes, my brother,
Ask him to do all I'd have done:
make him your leader.
I'm going now. A place I have to go.
Do all I ask, and pray for me that soon
you'll hear my pain is done, my soul's at peace.   740
(Exit. Music.)

CHORUS
   Skin prickles,
heart thuds,
wings of longing;
Pan, eeoh Pan,
you make Olympus dance,
cross seas for us,
dance with us, dance with us.
Apollo, lord of Delos,
cross seas for us,
dance with us, dance with us.   750

   Pain gone,
tears gone,
joy's born for us.
Zeus, eeoh Zeus.
Lord Ajax turns to God,
turns back to God,
in the fullness of time,
forgets his anger,
in the fullness of time.
All's possible, it comes!   760
(Music ends. Enter Soldier.)

SOLDIER

News, friends!
Teucer is here,
fresh from the hills of Mysia.
Listen! They're shouting at him,
every Greek in camp.
He's marching through the army
to find the generals, he's surrounded.
on all sides, soldiers
jostling him, shouting insults.
"That madman's brother,   770
that traitor's brother,
stone him, pulp him, smash him."
Hands on swords, blades drawn,
it flared to the limit.
The old men stopped it,
put a stop to it: talk, not blood.
Where's Ajax? This affects our master:
he needs to hear.

CHORUS

He's gone.
Took himself off.   780
Something new:
he's planning something new.

SOLDIER

Eeoo!
Too late, I've taken too long to get here.
They sent me here too late.

CHORUS

Too late for what? We've done all we could.

SOLDIER

Teucer said, he was to be kept inside,
not go out, till His Honor was here himself.

CHORUS
　　Well, he's gone. Wiser, saner:
　　to make his peace with gods he scorned.   790

SOLDIER
　　Then he's a fool. If Calchas is right,
　　if the prophet's right, he's lost what wits he had.

CHORUS
　　What d'you mean? What are you here to tell us?

SOLDIER
　　Only what I know because I was there.
　　Calchas broke away from the generals,
　　where the sons of Atreus couldn't hear him;
　　took Teucer's hand, insisted, as a friend:
　　"This above all, do all you can,
　　keep Ajax out of sight,
　　all day, out of sight inside his quarters.   800
　　If you want him alive, don't let him out.
　　Athena's rage is after him,
　　but for this day only, for this one day:
　　It'll be spent by nightfall."

　　"We think too much," the prophet said.
　　"We humans, we aim too high, and when we do
　　Gods jump on us, pour pain on us and ditch us.
　　We're mortal; we should never look higher."
　　That's what Ajax did, lord Ajax,
　　on the day he left home, left his wits behind,   810
　　left all his father told him. Wise advice.
　　"Conquer all you like," the old man told him,
　　"but remember, with God's help always."
　　And what did he answer, Mr. Bigmouth answer?
　　"God's help?" he had to say.
　　"Any booby wins big prizes
　　if gods are with him.

Trust me, father:
my path to glory's mine,
I don't need help."   820

Same story, time and again.
Athena told him once, Our Lady Athena:
"On, on! You're doing well!
Blood hands! Fight on!"
He had to answer back, brag when he shouldn't.
"Madam, find someone else to strengthen.
The other Greeks need you.
Where Ajax stands, the line holds firm,
no enemy breaks through, not ever."
That's what he said. The goddess' rage,   830
he brought it on himself.
Who forgives a man who plays the superman?

Never mind. He's at risk today. One day:
if he survives today, with God's good help
we can save him yet. That's what Calchas said.
That's what Teucer sent me here to tell you.
"Watch Ajax well," he said.
And now it's too late, you say?
In that case, if Calchas was right,
our hero is no more.   840

CHORUS
      Tecmessa, child of misery,
      come, see this man. Hear what he says.
      New pain: the razor strips the flesh.
(Enter Tecmessa with Eurysaces.)

TECMESSA
      I thought it was over.
      Inside, I was resting.
      Must I get up?
      More wretchedness?

CHORUS
>*He* came. Hear him.
>Ajax and his fate. It hurts to hear.

TECMESSA
>Oee moee.   850
>Soldier, what is it?
>Is it over?

SOLDIER
>For you, I don't know.
>For Ajax, if he's out,
>if he's disappeared, it's bad.

TECMESSA
>He *has* gone out.
>What d'you mean?
>It hurts to ask.

SOLDIER
>Teucer's orders:
>keep the man inside,   860
>don't let him out alone.

TECMESSA
>Where is lord Teucer?
>Why these orders?

SOLDIER
>He's just arrived. And he's afraid.
>If Ajax isn't here,
>if he's gone out alone, he's dead.

TECMESSA
>Oee moee. I can't bear it.
>Who told him so?

SOLDIER

> The prophet, Calchas. Today
> is life or death for him, he says.   870

TECMESSA

> Oee goh. Friends, stop it,
> the unstoppable, stop it.
> Run to Teucer, bring him. Hurry.
> And you: search the beach for Ajax,
> you go west, you east. Find him.
> Wherever he is, oh, find him.
> I see it now. He cheated me.
> what love I had, I have no more.
> Oee moee. Child, darling,
> what can I do? I can't sit here.   880
> Go with them, as far as I can,
> go with them. Hurry, hurry.
> Don't dawdle. We have to save
> a man who longs to die.

CHORUS

> I'm ready. Deeds now, not words.
> Fast as we can. We're here. We're coming.
> *(Exeunt omnes.)*

SCENE TWO

(Another, remote part of the shore. Enter Ajax, alone. He carries his sword and sets it in the sand, point upward.)

AJAX

> The killer blade stands ready.
> Point up. As if I'd time to care.
> Lord Hector's gift, the man I detested most,
> whose sight I loathed. Stuck firm,   890
> here in our enemies' sand, I spit on it,
> new-sharpened, firmly fixed,

a blade I trust to bring me quick to death.
I'm ready. Zeus, hear me:
one favor only, one little thing, no more.
Tell Teucer, send a messenger,
cruel news. Let him be first, lift my body,
spiked here on this newly-blooded blade.
If enemies see me first, I'm carrion:
meat for dogs, for birds. Zeus, hear me.   900
Let Hermes, escort of souls, grant instant sleep,
sword rips my heart, one little jump
from life to death, no more.

Avenging Furies, help me,
grave Furies who bestride the world,
forever virgin, who supervise all mortal pain,
witness. The sons of Atreus have destroyed my life
evil for evil, snatch them down to Hell,
let them die as I do now. Come now!
Be quick, be just, and glut yourselves on Greeks.   910

Sun above, your chariot rides the sky,
when you see my native land, ease golden reins,
tell them my misery, what fate was mine.
The old man my father, the mother who nursed me—
poor lady! She'll hear the news,
our whole city will hear her shrieks.

No tears. What's gained by whining?
Time to do it. Now. Be quick.
Look, Death, Death, look: I'm here.
Time to talk when we're face to face below.   920
Light of day, sky-dazzle,
sun in your chariot above,
farewell. Sweet light, farewell,
dear Salamis, farewell,
my rock, my hearth, my home,

great Athens, mother of heroes,
rivers and streams of Troy, Troy's fields,
farewell. You fed me; I leave you.
These are Ajax' last words on earth:
whatever else I say only the Dead will hear.   930
(He falls on his sword. Music. Enter Chorus, in separate groups.)

CHORUS
     On. On.
     Keep looking.
     Where? Where?
     I've looked everywhere.
     No sign of him.
     What's that?
     Someone shouting.
     Shipmates, there you are.
     Any news?
     We've searched every inch,   940
     west of the ships.
     Any luck?
     If aching eyes are luck!
     Nothing to the east.
     He's vanished.
     Who'll tell us where he is?
     A fisherman, perhaps,
     hard-working, all night awake?
     A mountain-nymph, a water-sprite,
     have they seen him, wandering, cursing?   950
     Can they tell us where he is?
     We're drifting,
     expert sailors, rudderless:
     he's sick, why can't we see him?

TECMESSA *(off)*
     Eeoh moee moee.

CHORUS
  There, in the trees,
  someone shouting.

TECMESSA *(off)*
  Eeoh t-lee-mohn.

CHORUS
  Tecmessa.
  His war-prize.   960
  His woman.
  Collapsed in tears.
  What is it?
(Enter Tecmessa.)

TECMESSA
  Dead. Gone. All gone.
  I'm dead. Oh, help me.

CHORUS
  What's happened?

TECMESSA
  Ajax, our Ajax.
  Over there.
  Blood bubbling.
  Sword, sword in the heart.   970

CHORUS
  Oh moee.
  Who'll lead us home?
  Oh moee.
  Dead, lord, we're dead,
  your crew, all slaughtered.
  Why, lord, why?
  Poor lady, we weep for you.

TECMESSA
Nothing left but tears.

CHORUS
Who did it? Who ended him?

TECMESSA
His own hand. He did.   980
Sword stuck in the sand,
point upward. He fell on it.
Over there. He fell on it.

CHORUS
Oh moee.
We shut our eyes, we lost him,
the master we loved, we did it.
Blind we were. Knew nothing.
We should have thought.
Show me. Poor lord, poor Ajax,
cursed by God, where is he?   990

TECMESSA
No one must see him.
Who could bear it? We loved him.
I'll cover him. Blood, heart's blood,
fountains of blood, he stabbed himself,
crimson wells from his chest,
from his nostrils, he did it, did it.

Oee moee.
What can I do?
Who'll lift you?
Where's Teucer?   1000
He'll hold you in his arms,
make you neat for death,
your brother, your dear one.

Ajax, O Ajax, to have come to this,
Even enemies see this, and weep.

CHORUS
Dear lord, you destroyed yourself.
Grim face, stubborn eyes,
tongue cursing them, cursing them,
the sons of Atreus who betrayed you,
bitterness, darkness of heart,   1010
you brought it on yourself.
That golden armor,
Achilles' armor, it ended you,
you fought for it, it killed you.

TECMESSA
Eeoh moee moee.

CHORUS
Pain stabs her.
Tears scald for him.

TECMESSA
Eoh moee moee.

CHORUS
Tecmessa,
weep for him.   1020
You loved him.
You weep for him.
Who'll blame you?

TECMESSA
Words. You're words.
And I all pain, all tears.

CHORUS
We weep for you.

TECMESSA

Oh moee.

Our son, our baby,

who'll take us,

who'll own us now?   1030

CHORUS

Oh moee.

All pain is yours.

Oh moee.

They'll hurt you,

the sons of Atreus,

hurt you.

God save you, save you.

TECMESSA

What happened here: God's work.

CHORUS

God trampled you, God hurt you.

TECMESSA

She did it. Zeus' daughter,   1040

Athena, our Lady,

grim-faced Athena,

she did it to please Odysseus.

CHORUS

Feoo feoo.

How he frowned for this,

ate out his heart for this.

He's laughing, hear him laughing—

our lord made mad, made dead,

and Odysseus laughing,

the sons of Atreus laughing.   1050

(Music ends.)

TECMESSA
>Let them laugh.
>They wanted him dead, let them laugh.
>and tomorrow, when they long for him,
>when the battle gets hard and they long for him,
>let them laugh at him then, let them cry for him.
>A fool has diamonds in his hand,
>he spends them like pebbles—
>and as soon as they're gone, he cries for them.
>Ajax is dead. I'm destroyed, they laugh.
>He has what he wants. He prayed for this,   1060
>he hugged it to him: to die when he chose,
>to be left to choose. Are they to laugh at that?
>He owed his death to God, not them; he paid it.
>Odysseus, your triumph is water in your hands.
>You've lost him. Lord Ajax is lost to you—
>he's gone, he's abandoned me, I weep, I weep.

TEUCER (*off*)
>Eeoh moee moee.

CHORUS
>Hush. Someone weeping.
>Lord Teucer, weeping.
>He's here. He knows.   1070
>(*Enter Teucer.*)

TEUCER
>O Ajax, brother,
>All life to me . . . you're dead,
>they say you're dead . . .

CHORUS
>Lord Ajax is dead, my lord.

TEUCER
>Oh moee. Fate crushes me.

CHORUS
As things now are . . .

TEUCER
How can I bear it?

CHORUS
Tears of misery . . .

TEUCER
Snatched from me, snatched from me . . .

CHORUS
Weep, lord.   1080

TEUCER
Feoo talass.
The child. Where's the child?
Where is he?

CHORUS
Left there in camp.

TEUCER
Fetch him, now.
A lion's cub, its father dead,
its mother bereft . . . They'll kill him,
his enemies will kill him.
(to Tecmessa)
Fetch him. Quick about it.
When a great one's down,   1090
the whole world runs to kick him.
(Exit Tecmessa.)

CHORUS
Good work, my lord.
When our lord was alive,
he asked that you take the child.

TEUCER
    Of all the sights I've seen,
    this hurts the most.
    Of all the paths I've walked,
    none blistered me like this.
    O Ajax, brother, my dear,
    I was trying to find you,   1100
    looking everywhere,
    when I heard the news.
    Shrill rumor ran—
    some god behind it—
    from Greek to Greek.
    "Ajax is gone. Ajax is dead."
    Only a rumor:
    out there, I choked my sobs.
    But now . . . the truth.
    I see it, it tears my heart.   1110

    Oee moee.
    You: uncover him, show me the worst.
(An attendant enters and uncovers Ajax.)
    Cold eyes. Cruel sight. Bitter bravery:
    the poison seed you've sown,
    and I must reap.
    Where can I go? Who'll smile on me?
    When you needed help, where was I?
    Not here, not here.
    Imagine Telamon, our father:
    how will he welcome me   1120
    when I come home and you lie dead?
    Good news never made him smile.
    He'll lash me with words,
    badmouth the bastard
    he got on some whore he won in war:
    the traitor, me, the coward, me,

who let sweet Ajax die.
Trickster he'll call me,
he'll say I plotted this,
to let you die, his heir,   1130
to snatch your place.
That's what he'll say, our father,
he's sour with age, he's hungry to be crossed.
He'll throw me out:
no land, no name, a slave.

My welcome home.
And here in Troy? What's here for me?
What's dear to me? Only you, only you.
In enemies, I'm rich.

Oee moee. What now?   1140
Rip you from the barb of this bright skewer?
Poor Ajax, to die this way!
He did this—can't you see?
Hector, dead Hector,
He lifted his hand from beyond the grave,
you died. When you fought him before,
a duel before the army, both stayed your hands,
the pair of you, gave each other
gifts of honor: a belt, a sword.
Gifts of honor, gifts of death!   1150
Sweet gods, two men, one fate!
Hector, lashed to Achilles' chariot—
by what? The belt you gave him!
Mangled, shredded, he breathed no more.
And here's the sword he gave you:
you fell and died on it.
Some Fury forged this blade,
lord Hades crafted that belt,
who has the killing skill.

Gods planned this, did this.   1160
Gods pattern all human lives.
That's what I say. You don't agree?
Think what you like, and so will I.

CHORUS
No more words, my lord.
Find somewhere to bury him.
In secret. Tell no one.
Our enemy's coming.
What is it he wants?
He did what he did to us—
Has he come to gloat?   1170

TEUCER
Who is it? Some army man?

CHORUS
Menelaus. The one we sailed for.

TEUCER
Oh yes. Close to: no mistaking him.
(Enter Menelaus, attended by soldiers.)

MENELAUS
You.
Leave him where he lies.
No honor guard. Leave him.
This is an order.

TEUCER
Whose order?

MENELAUS
Mine. And my brother's,
the Supreme Commander's.   1180

TEUCER
   What reason? If you don't mind me asking?

MENELAUS
   As follows.
   Hope was, he'd come from home,
   friend and ally to the Greeks.
   Instead, more trouble than all the Trojans.
   Plotted to kill the whole damn army,
   night attack, spear in hand.
   Some god put paid to that,
   else we'd all be lying dead where he is now,
   and he'd be living. As it was, luck was,   1190
   God turned his treachery on sheep and cows.

   That's the reason.
   No grave permitted:
   he's to be chucked on the sand
   for gulls to pick at.
   Orders, official: don't get ideas.
   Don't try to stop us, he's in our hands.
   We couldn't control him alive,
   we'll do it now he's dead.
   No respect,   1200
   never did a thing I told him.

   Men of lower rank must learn:
   a general's here to be obeyed.
   If laws are to be kept,
   societies survive, we need the rule of fear.
   Armies too: the chain of command.
   shield and buckler: respect and fear.
   Every soldier, big as you like,
   has to learn: step out of line, he's done!
   Fear's the ticket, respect is the spur,   1210
   learn that, no trouble.

But get above yourself,
start doing as you like, what then?
Ship of state, breezing along,
calm as calm, down it goes, the bottom.
Fear's essential, keeps things on course.
No use thinking we can do as we choose:
we pay the price for that, it hurts.

Things come and go.
How big he was, how hot he was!   1220
Now I'm in charge. So, orders:
he's not to be buried. Try it,
and you'll lie down there beside him.

CHORUS

Menelaus, what you say is wise.
But be careful, lord: respect the Dead.

TEUCER

"Don't get above yourself!"
He reminds me who he is
and who I am,
and this is what he says!
Let's start again, at the beginning.   1230
You say he was *your* ally?
Your doing, to fetch him here to Troy?
He was captain of his ship,
these men, his fellow-countrymen,
were his to command.
Over him, over them, you'd no authority.
You, king of Sparta, are you lord of Salamis?
Then was my brother king in Sparta?
What, *you* rule Ajax? You were equals:
both kings, both answerable to others—   1240
Supreme commander!

Go back to your own men.
Bang out orders there,
tell *them* what to do, "or else."
I'll bury my brother:
the laws of the gods demand it,
and neither of you will stop me,
not you, not that twin of yours.
Twin general—I'm not afraid of you.
D'you think lord Ajax   1250
came to Troy for your sake,
to fetch back that wife of yours?
Only slaves did that, your drudges.
My brother swore an oath,
swore an oath and kept it;
you, to him, were nothing.

So come here all you like,
your men, your C-in-C, your clatter.
I won't even look round. Who are you?

CHORUS
   Be careful, lord.   1260
   Things are bad,
   why make them worse?
   You're right, maybe, but don't overdo it.

MENELAUS
   What are you? A bigmouth? And a *bowman*?

TEUCER
   And proud of it.

MENELAUS
   Give you a warrior's gear,
   there'd be no stopping you.

TEUCER
   Stark naked, I'd still beat *you*.

MENELAUS

    If boasts had muscles, you'd have me shaking.

TEUCER

    My strength: I speak for justice.   1270

MENELAUS

    Oh, justice! He killed us, you honor him?

TEUCER

    He killed you? What, come to life again?

MENELAUS

    So far as *he's* concerned, I'm dead. God saved me.

TEUCER

    The god you dishonor now?

MENELAUS

    How dishonor? I keep God's law.

TEUCER

    "Bury the dead"—God's law. You say, "I won't."

MENELAUS

    We're to bury our enemies? Unheard of.

TEUCER

    Your enemy? When did he *challenge* you?

MENELAUS

    We loathed each other. As you damned well know.

TEUCER

    So you rigged a vote and stole his honor.   1280

MENELAUS

    Blame the judges for that. Not up to me.

TEUCER

Oh, clever.

Do good men down, then wriggle out of it.

MENELAUS

Big words, big trouble on the way.

TEUCER

For someone, yes: big trouble.

MENELAUS

Get this: no burial. Denied.

TEUCER

And you get this: he'll be buried. Now.

MENELAUS

I'm thinking of a captain,

another bigmouth,

who sent his sailors to sea in a gathering storm,   1290

and when winds began to howl, waves roared,

where was he? Huddling in his cloak,

biting his lip while his men fell over him.

See what I'm getting at? You're all words now,

but a breeze is blowing, a storm is brewing,

huff and puff all you like, it'll blow you away.

TEUCER

I'm thinking of a windbag,

a brainless windbag,

who trampled his comrades, his suffering comrades,

made them nothing. And a passing stranger—   1300

just like me, it could have been me—

saw what was happening, took him aside

and said, "Don't insult the dead;

if you do, you'll be sorry." Fair warning,

more than the oaf deserved.

If the cap fits, wear it. Get the point?

MENELAUS

> I'm going. Bandy words with you?
> Beneath my dignity. No chance:
> when I say jump, you jump.

TEUCER

> Tail between your legs. Beneath *my* dignity.   1310
> A donkey brays, and I stand listening.

(Exeunt Menelaus and soldiers.)

CHORUS

> He won't leave it there.
> He's going to make trouble.
> Teucer, don't waste time.
> Bury your brother—any grave will do.
> Honor forever, last resting-place—go, now.

TEUCER

> They're here, just in time: his son, his woman.
> They'll add their tears; they'll honor him.

(Enter Tecmessa with attendant women and Eurysaces.)

> Child, come closer.
> Touch him. Pray for him.   1320
> Your father. Three strands of hair:
> yours, hers, mine. Take them,
> kneel with them, offer them,
> grave-gifts. Ask his help with them.
> And if Greeks come, lay hands on you,
> rough hands, drag you from this duty,
> God send them death in exile,
> no burial, no heirs,
> God cut off their future
> as I cut off these hairs.   1330
> Here, boy, hold them tight,
> kneel down, don't let anyone move you.

Women, be men. Stand by him, guard him.
I'll dig a grave. I'll see to it: I'll not be stopped.
(*Exit. Music.*)

CHORUS
　　When will it end?
　　Storm-wandering,
　　blood-toil for Troy,
　　our shame, our pain,
　　our agony for Troy?

　　He brought us here,   1340
　　stirred war for us,
　　yoked death for us,
　　all shame, all pain—
　　he did it, he lived to do it.

　　No crowns, flowers, dancing,
　　no throbbing of flutes, no wine,
　　he stole all joy from us.
　　No rest, sweet in night's arms,
　　no women, oh moee,
　　we toss and turn,   1350
　　cold beds, dew soaks us,
　　Troy haunts us, haunts us.

　　Our lord could have saved us,
　　saved us from nightmare,
　　Ajax, spearlord, saved us.
　　He's gone. Grim gods of death
　　have stolen all joy from us.
　　Oh, weep for home,
　　for Sounion, for Salamis,
　　for Athens, oh, for Athens.   1360
(*Music ends. Enter Teucer.*)

TEUCER

    I ran, ran back. Agamemnon's coming.
    He's angry. He isn't going to spare us.
(Enter Agamemnon.)

AGAMEMNON

    It's you, then, is it? Who d'you think you are?
    Shout off your mouth and get away with it?
    Son-of-a-whore! Imagine
    if you'd had a proper mother:
    you'd be yelling on stilts,
    no stopping you. As it is,
    Mister Nobody pleads for Mister Nothing.
    We're not in charge? Don't command the fleet,   1370
    the Greeks, the army, *you?*
    That's what you say? His own man, Ajax?
    Big boasts from a slave, big trouble.

    What did he amount to, the man you brag about?
    That big high-flier? Was I not higher?
    Sole champion of Greece? It comes to this:
    we made a fair decision, a majority decision
    about Achilles' armor, and you cry foul.
    Is that how it's going to be for always?
    You disagree, the rest of us give way   1380
    in case you lurk and sulk and stab us in the back?
    Stand for that, and what won't we stand for?
    If honest victors are shouldered out
    and the losers announce they've won,
    what law survives? Don't even answer.
    We don't need thugs, big shoulders,
    brains are what we need, the long view, sanity.
    One little goad, the big ox keeps the road.

    Which will apply to you, unless you listen up.
    The man is dead, a shadow, and you strut about,   1390

let your tongue run where it likes—bad idea.
Remember who you are. If you've got a case,
find a freeborn warrior to make it.
This babble of yours, this blah-blah-blah:
it's nothing to me. I don't know who you are.

CHORUS

Both of you, compromise:
that's best, now and always.

TEUCER

Feoo.
How soon we forget the dead.
How quickly gratitude drains away.
Only treachery remains.   1400
O Ajax, do you hear him now?
"Ajax? Remind me who he was."
This from the man you, time and again,
risked your life to reach out and save.
Forget it. Yesterday? It's gone.

(to Agamemnon)

You're babbling. All of it, nonsense.
You've forgotten. The day you were trapped,
fenced in, a rabbit in the snares of war,
Who came running, alone?
Fire leaping to the mastheads,   1410
scorching the decks,
and Hector, rampant,
skipping the trenches
and pounding on the ships—
who stopped him? Ajax,
admit it, Ajax, the one you call "criminal."
He did it, he did it, the one you say
was "no high-flier" compared to you.
faced Hector, one to one as Fate decreed.
Forget about orders, he was in there,   1420

fast, in the thick of it. The chips were down.
Big shoulders, an ox, a lump of clay?
Out leapt his challenge,
like a name from a hat, the first to go.

He did what he did—and I was with him,
The slave-whore's son, Mister Blah-blah-blah.
Look me in the eye when you say those things.
Who was Pelops, your father's father?
A blah-blah Phrygian.
Your father Atreus—what did he stew   1430
to make his brother's dinner? His brother's children.
Who was your mother? Some Cretan twinkie
her Dad found at it with some blah-blah-blah
and packed her off to feed the fishes.
They tell no tales.

What are you, that you call me slave?
My father was Telamon,
his prize for supreme courage
my mother in his bed.
A princess, Laomedon's daughter,   1440
Heracles presented her, gift of all gifts.
I'm the best, born of the best—
and I'm to disown my blood,
let you chuck him out, unburied?
Well, shame on you. And get this clear:
dishonor him, dishonor all three of us,
his wife, his son, his brother.
I'll die for him, far happier to die for him
than for that woman of yours—
I'm sorry, your brother! Look in the mirror,   1450
don't look at me. You'll find out.
Be smart. Back off. Don't do it with me.
(Enter Odysseus.)

CHORUS
> Lord Odysseus, welcome.
> If you've come to help,
> that tongue of yours,
> not make things worse, you're welcome.

ODYSSEUS
> Agamemnon, what is it?
> Menelaus, then you,
> shouting, yelling
> above this gallant corpse—   1460
> I could hear you clear across camp.

AGAMEMNON
> And him?
> Did you hear what *he* was saying—
> my dear Odysseus,
> what *he* was saying?
> Insufferable!

ODYSSEUS
> Well, now,
> if a man's insulted and answers back,
> Who'll blame him?

AGAMEMNON
> No insults. A reprimand. For disobedience.   1470

ODYSSEUS
> What disobedience, exactly?

AGAMEMNON
> I gave clear orders: no burial.
> And he says he will. He's planning it!

ODYSSEUS
> You're an old friend. We pull together.
> Nothing's changed. Listen to me.

AGAMEMNON
> I'd be a fool if I didn't.
> Odysseus—who matters more to me?

ODYSSEUS
> Listen, then. In God's name, bury him!
> What are you thinking of?
> You're blind with hate. Deny him burial   1480
> and trample justice! I loathed him,
> more than any other Greek in camp.
> I detested all he was—and still I say
> he was the bravest man I ever saw,
> except for Achilles, the best and bravest
> who ever came to Troy. Admit it!
> Justice demands! If you shame him
> you smear God's law. Hate him or love him,
> he was an honorable man; you owe him honor.

AGAMEMNON
> My Odysseus, you take his side in this?   1490

ODYSSEUS
> When hating was right, I hated him.

AGAMEMNON
> Kick him aside. He's carrion!

ODYSSEUS
> This is petty-minded, lord.

AGAMEMNON
> I'm in command. I make the rules.

ODYSSEUS
When friends give wise advice—

AGAMEMNON
When friends forget their place—

ODYSSEUS
The advice is mine, the decision yours.

AGAMEMNON
I remind you again who it is you fight for.

ODYSSEUS
An enemy, a warrior.

AGAMEMNON
Your enemy's dead, and now you fawn on him!   1500

ODYSSEUS
Since he deserves respect.

AGAMEMNON
You're just like the rest.
Wind changes, you change your tune.

ODYSSEUS
People change.
Friends into enemies, for instance.

AGAMEMNON
Not *my* friends.

ODYSSEUS
You'd rather have stubbornness? Not me.

AGAMEMNON
So *I'm* to cave in? Look weak?

ODYSSEUS
　　A beacon of justice, true Greek justice.

AGAMEMNON
　　I'm to order this burial? You insist on that?   1510

ODYSSEUS
　　As someone will one day insist for me.

AGAMEMNON
　　This is about Odysseus?

ODYSSEUS
　　My lord, who else?

AGAMEMNON
　　Well: you take the blame for it.

ODYSSEUS
　　You take the credit.

AGAMEMNON
　　For friendship's sake, your sake—
　　not for him, oh not for him:
　　he remains our enemy forever.
　　So be it. See to it.
(Exit.)

CHORUS
　　You play to win, Odysseus.   1520
　　Only fools would doubt it.

ODYSSEUS
　　Teucer, hear me:
　　your enemy before, and now your friend.
　　I'll help you bury him, a hero's grave,
　　pay last respects. He's earned it.

TEUCER
> Odysseus, thank you.
> What else can I say?
> I misjudged you.
> I thought you hated him,
> and here you stand up for him,   1530
> when everyone comes to kick him.
> That lunatic our leader,
> and his brother, who'd have let him rot,
> who'd have left him here.
> God punish them, avenging Furies,
> Justice who brings all to pass,
> stamp them down,
> pay what they've earned
> for what they've done . . .
>
> Odysseus,   1540
> noble son of a noble father,
> I'm embarrassed,
> but he wouldn't have you touch him . . .
> As for the rest, you're welcome,
> and anyone else you bring,
> it's up to you. You've been good to us,
> a friend in need. But let me see to him.

ODYSSEUS
> I'd have been glad to help.
> But whatever you say . . .
> I'll go.   1550

(Exit.)

TEUCER
> It's over.
> No time to waste.
> You men, start digging.
> Hurry.
> You, heat water,

make him neat for death.
You others, from the tent,
his armor: fetch it.

Child, help me.
You're strong enough.   1560
Touch him: don't be afraid.
Help me move him.
Gently.
Blood pours from him still,
strength pours from him . . .

Gather round,
pay respect.
You loved him.
He was honest and just,
he was a perfect man.   1570

CHORUS
    We're mortal. All things
    are ours to understand
    save one: our future.
    We'll know it when it comes.
End of the play

Women of Trachis

Translated by
Brendan Galvin

From title to final sentence, *Women of Trachis* has been regarded as a "problem" play. Although the play is named for the chorus, it is generally agreed that the choric odes are unremarkable and add little to the dramatic action. Whether it belongs to Sophocles' early, middle, or late period has also been debated, but the major critical question has been whether Deianira or her husband Heracles is its tragic figure. She is the focus of the first two-thirds of the action, while he and his death occupy the final third of the play. They are never on stage at the same time, and if the play's subject is Deianira's unstinting love and the tragic mistake resulting from that love, she dies too soon, leaving Heracles suffering in a denouement that may seem contrived. If, on the other hand, Heracles is the play's focus, he is too long in making his appearance and too little present, and the subtler character of his wife steals the drama. These, and a hundred other questions and qualifications, have dogged the play's critical reception. Some have even doubted that Sophocles wrote it.

It makes little sense to ascribe such issues to ineptness on Sophocles' part. He was, after all, one of the fathers of dramatic technique as we know it, the originator of the triangular scene in which three actors speak (as in Deianira's stichomythic dialogue with the Messenger and Lichas), and a master of characterization as well. Rather than criticize *Women of Trachis* for what it isn't and what it doesn't do, we should be concerned with the dramatist's limning of character, for that is what makes the play succeed far better than is sometimes recognized.

In Deianira and Heracles we have two diametrically opposed figures. Deianira embodies the qualities we attribute to domesticity. Among other things, she is concerned for the safety of her husband, children, and household. She is compassionate for others, even the young captive Iole who has replaced her as the object of Heracles' love. Concerned with keeping her good reputation, she is also wisely understanding of how beauty can cause pain. The cluster of images Sophocles attributes to her includes many references to home, the marriage bed, and the nursing of children. Her reasonable qualities are conveyed in her speech rhythms as well, narratives delivered in long, thoughtful sentences.

Heracles, on the other hand, speaks in staccato outbursts much of the time, in part because he is in great pain, but also because his nature is impulsive and aggressive. Totally self-involved, he is so unconcerned for his wife and family that for more than a year he hasn't bothered to inform them of his whereabouts. When told she is dead, he shows no sorrow. He is a threat to his own domesticity as well as that of others, especially when he is driven by lust for another man's daughter, and he treats his son Hyllus as a test-case for his own genetic makeup.

Heracles' reputation as the consummate warrior is likely to make him an unsympathetic figure for our time, and indeed the conflict of character between him and Deianira may appeal to the contemporary reader on the level of pop psychology: "Men are from Mars, women are from Venus." And who better than Deianira illustrates our current fascination with why bad things happen to good people? Again, parallels could be drawn between the events in this play and the aftermath of our own Cold War. When long-time military activity ceases to have an adequate outlet, it can turn on its own social fabric, as in the Oklahoma City bombing and the formation of private militias. *Women of Trachis* is a tragedy of character, then, with Deianira and Heracles representing opposed attitudes that cannot coexist in the domestic space Sophocles established for the working out of his drama.

The character of Hyllus is of paramount importance as well. We see him first as a feckless youth with no thought for the fates of his parents, but in the course of the action he becomes a man. Hyllus shows some of the courage of his father in standing up to him. He accepts the responsibility Heracles places on him in arranging for the funeral pyre and in the promise to marry Iole, whom he regards as his worst enemy. In this final action he also reveals himself as the compassionate and forgiving son of Deianira, and it is with him that the reader sympathizes, since he accepts the weight of an adult world that is unreasonable and therefore tragic. Ultimately, he provides a return to moral balance, and, fittingly, he has the last word: "There is nothing here that is not Zeus." In this exchange between Hyllus and Heracles the contemporary reader may recognize a further point of comparison with our own time: Heracles, diminished as a man and in incurable pain, asks his son to help him die. This may be the earliest reference in literature to the moral questions surrounding assisted suicide.

Women of Trachis is also notable for the way Sophocles quickly changes his characters' fortunes. He prepares us for this in the parodos,

> Neither the shimmering night,
> nor misfortune, nor riches
> remain for men, but fly to other men
> for them to know happiness and its loss.
> Expect this always, O Queen,
> keep it in mind. (128–33)

In the shaky world of this play certitude is nonexistent, instability the norm, as witness Deianira's rapid shifts from fear to joy and back again on learning of Heracles' safety, and then that he has sent Iole home to be his bedmate, then that Nessus' magic may assure Heracles' love, then that the clump of wool dissolved in sunlight, and so on.

Again, the play is Sophoclean in its construction around opposites: light and darkness, pain and joy, the past and the present, feminine and masculine, disease and healing, love and lust, monstrous and human, the old world of courageous energy and the newer one of domesticity. Such polarities, when added to the shifting fortunes of its characters, make *Women of Trachis* a drama of action in a world vibrating with tensions.

In making this translation I have been guided by Ezra Pound's proscription that a poet should never say anything that he couldn't, "in some circumstance, in the stress of some emotion, actually say." This seems particularly necessary in translating a play, and especially one containing the dramatic tenor of Heracles' dialogue, which could easily spill over into the bathetic. The question of decorum has everywhere been a consideration, since *Women of Trachis* is a tragedy, and I have steered away from both a too-informal colloquial speech and an overly dramatic one, in order to present a readable version to a contemporary American audience. Like every translator, I hope the result is a symbiosis, a living together of two organisms whose association is mutually beneficial.

DEIANIRA, wife of Heracles
NURSE
HYLLUS, son of Heracles and Deianira
CHORUS of young women of Trachis
MESSENGER
LICHAS, herald of Heracles
OLD MAN
HERACLES, Greek hero, son of Zeus
NONSPEAKING
  Servants, attendants
  Iole, young captive woman, daughter of Eurytus
  Women of Oechalia, captives of Heracles

*(The house of Deianira and Heracles in Trachis. Deianira enters
from the house, followed by the Nurse.)*

DEIANIRA
  You cannot call a life happy or sad
  before its final day—so the wise have said
  from the beginning of time.
  As for my life: burdened with sorrow
  from birth to death. That will tell it all.
  Even in Pleuron, a girl in the house
  of my father Oeneus, I was more terrified
  of marrying than any other woman
  in Aetolia. The reason was Achelous,
  that river of three shapes, desirous   10
  of my hand. First he appeared to my father
  as a bull, then coiled as a shimmering
  snake, then as a bull-faced man
  whose tangled beard splattered waterfalls.
  Imagine a marriage bed with that

waiting in it! Always I prayed for death
to take me from that consummation.
At last there came the famous Heracles,
born of Alcmene and Zeus. He struggled
with Achelous and overcame that thing,   20
rescuing me. How, I cannot say,
though a mere spectator might. Overwhelmed
because my beauty seemed to be the source
of all my pain, I hid myself
from their fight. Zeus the warlord
assured the victory, if victory it was.
Since then, as Heracles' bedmate,
I have nourished all my fears for him,
each night new ones arriving
before the others are weaned and gone.   30
The children we had he visits now
as a farmer will visit a distant field,
only at planting and at gathering times.
That's been his life, home for awhile,
then gone again, called to another master.
Now all his duties have been labored through,
but I'm more terrified than before.
Exiles here in Trachis, his family depends
on strangers, all because he murdered
Iphitus. And where is Heracles?   40
Gone again, my terror for him standing
in his place. There's trouble,
I can feel it. A year at first, then more,
and not a word in all that time?
The tablet he left with me portends
deepening pain, I'm sure of it.
May it not increase my pain, O Gods.

NURSE

How often have I looked on as you lamented,
desolate over Heracles' absences,

O Deianira, and never offered a word!   50
But you are my mistress and I am your slave,
and if I don't presume in this question,
why have you never sent a son—for you
have many—to ask after your husband?
Hyllus might be the one to choose,
provided that he's worried about his father.
Here he comes now, and in a hurry.
Take my advice if it seems wise to you
and send the boy to locate Heracles.
(Hyllus enters, moving with youthful energy, as if he's come from some
sport.)

DEIANIRA

My darling son, sometimes a slave can speak   60
as well as a free woman, and sometimes better.

HYLLUS

What has she said, Mother, if you can tell me?

DEIANIRA

That it's a disgrace—your father away so long,
and yet you haven't searched for him.

HYLLUS

But I know where he is, if the stories are true.

DEIANIRA

Where do your stories say he is?

HYLLUS

Plowing fields in Lydia this past year,
slave to a barbarian woman.

DEIANIRA

If they say that of him, anything might be said.

HYLLUS

But it's over with now, or so I hear.   70

DEIANIRA

Where is he, then? Is he living or dead?

HYLLUS

In Euboea, they claim, warring or readying
for war against Eurytus' city.

DEIANIRA

He left me a prophecy about that place.
Didn't you know of it, my son?

HYLLUS

I knew nothing, Mother. What prophecy?

DEIANIRA

It said he would die there now,
or if not, he'd have happiness
for all his days, once he'd performed this task.
Son, his future is being weighed. Go to him.   80
His future is ours, safety or ruin.

HYLLUS

Mother, I will. If I had known this prophecy
before, I would be with him now.
His luck is such, I never worried.
Now that I know there's danger, I'll stand
with him, until I know the truth.

DEIANIRA

Go then, Hyllus. Good news is always good,
whether we learn it early or late.
(Exit Hyllus. Enter Chorus.)

CHORUS
You are born out of the wreckage
of shimmering night   90
and bedded there afire—
O Sun, Sun! Where is Heracles,
Alcmene's child? Tell me,
I implore you, you fire-brilliance.
Is Heracles in the sea-straits,
or resting where the two continents
meet? You see everything, always.
I have heard that Deianira,
whom men have fought over,
is like a fearful bird   100
whose sleepless eyes
never cease worrying.
She nurses her fear with
the memory of Heracles' rovings,
even as she lies in misery
on their bed empty of him,
expecting bad news.

But her husband, of the line
of Cadmus, is pulled this way
and that, like waves moved   110
endlessly over the ocean,
first by the south wind, then
again by a wind from the north.
And yet he is always lifted
on a sea-swell powerful as those
on the ocean by Crete,
some god always rescues his descent
to the house of Death.
(Chorus addresses Deianira.)
That's why I scold you now.
Disagreeing, but with respect.   120
Do not allow all your hopes

to be erased. The omnipotent king
has ordained that we mortals
should suffer grief, and yet joy
and sorrow come to each of us
in their turn, the way the Bear arrives
and leaves on his starry track.

Neither the shimmering night,
nor misfortune, nor riches
remain for men, but fly to other men   130
for them to know happiness and its loss.
Expect this always, O Queen,
keep it in mind. When has Zeus
ever neglected his children?

DEIANIRA

News of my suffering has brought you here.
May you never learn my heartache from your own.
You are like the innocent girl who grows
in a safe place, protected from the sun,
the rain and the wind. Until she becomes
a woman her life is entirely a delight,   140
but then the darkness falls, full of
apprehension for her husband and children.
That's when the young thing would feel
my burdens. She'd understand them from her own.

Though I've cried over a lot of my life,
I'll tell you one grief deeper
than all the others. Before he departed
on this present journey, Heracles left me
an old tablet covered with a peculiar message.
This was the first time he'd mentioned   150
such a thing, though he'd gone away
to do battle so many times before,
and always to win, with no thought of dying.

This time, as though he foresaw his death,
he told me what—of all our property—
was mine, and how to divide our lands
among our sons. A year and three months,
he said, and he'd be dead, or else,
if he lived beyond that time, he'd have
a life free of struggle and sorrow.   160
The gods have assured it, he said,
an end to the labors of Heracles.
He had heard the sacred oak at Dodona
utter the same words through twin priestesses
called the Doves, and now is the time
they predicted. O friends, I burst from
my deepest sleeps afraid: I may have to go on
alone, without the best of all men.

CHORUS
    Let us speak of good things only,
        for here comes a laureled messenger to you.   170
(Enter Messenger.)

MESSENGER
    Deianira, I bring word that will free you
    from your worries, mistress. Heracles,
    Alcmene's son, has triumphed and returns
    with choice offerings for the gods.

DEIANIRA
    Old man, what are you saying to me?

MESSENGER
    Your husband shall be here soon,
    a greater hero than before he left.

DEIANIRA
    Did one who knows say this, or is it rumor?

MESSENGER

Lichas the herald says it to everyone
who's in the pasture with the cattle.   180
I hurried here as soon as I heard,
hoping for your gratitude. Or a reward perhaps?

DEIANIRA

If it's good news, why didn't Lichas himself bring it?

MESSENGER

The people of Malis have him surrounded, lady,
asking him this and that. He cannot make a path
through them, each one questioning him
until they're satisfied. He'd like to be here,
and he will, when he can pull himself away.
He'll be here soon, you'll see.

DEIANIRA

Zeus, lord of Oeta's unharvested meadow,   190
you have brought this long-awaited joy at last.
You women in the house, cry out!
And you outside! The sun I dared not hope for
has risen with this news. Its gladness warms us.

CHORUS

Cry out with joy for this house!
Cry out around its hearth, you girls
who shall be brides! Praise Apollo,
you men mingling among them,
praise the protecting arrow of Apollo!
Give thanks, you girls, and cry out   200
Artemis Ortygia's name, the stag-hunter,
sister of Apollo, bearer of twin torches!
Cry out the names of nymphs, our neighbors!
I have lifted my flute to play,
lord of my heart, and my joy is even deeper!

Ivy of the Bacchants' frenzy!
Give praise and see, Deianira,
look at what is before you!
(Enter Lichas, followed by the captive women, including Iole.)

DEIANIRA

Of course I see them, women,
my eyes, long watchful, could never miss this sight.   210
Welcome, Lichas, so long away! Welcome,
that is, if what you bring is welcome.

LICHAS

Lady, it's good to be here again,
and with such good news. All is well,
and my pleasure is doubled in telling you so.

DEIANIRA

Is Heracles alive? That's what I most want
to know, good man.

LICHAS

Not just alive, but increased in health
and strength when last I saw him.

DEIANIRA

Where? Abroad or in this land?   220

LICHAS

At Euboea, raising altars to Zeus
and making choice offerings from the harvest.

DEIANIRA

A vow he made? Or in obedience to an oracle.

LICHAS

A vow he made while battling to defeat
the country of these captive women here.

DEIANIRA

These unfortunate women. Who brings them here?
Unless I'm mistaken, they're to be pitied.

LICHAS

When he sacked Eurytus' city Heracles chose them
for himself and as gifts worthy of the gods.

DEIANIRA

Was it against Eurytus' city he was gone   230
so many days that I lost count of them?

LICHAS

No, most of those days he was in Lydia,
a bought slave—this he has said himself.
Zeus must have had a hand in it.
Bought by Omphale, the barbarian queen,
Heracles served her a whole year, as he has said,
in such disgrace he made himself a vow
that he'd enslave his own enslaver,
even the man's wife and children.
This was no idle promise, and once released,   240
he enlisted an army of foreigners
against Eurytus' city—Eurytus alone,
he said, was the cause of all his troubles.
Heracles had been welcomed to his hearth
in friendship, as before, but Eurytus
turned against him, raged like an angry sea,
claiming Heracles had used charmed arrows
to outshoot his sons at archery, then said
those sons would have prevailed in a fair contest.
Eurytus taunted him as a broken man,   250
a free-man's slave, then got him drunk
at banquet and threw him out his door.
This stung him more, so that when Iphitus,
Eurytus' son, came to the hill of Tiryns
searching for strayed horses, and dropped

his guard over some distraction, Heracles
threw him from the heights. It angered Zeus,
our father, who had Heracles sold into exile
and slavery for this one act of murderous deceit.
If he had fought Iphitus face-to-face,   260
surely Zeus would have forgiven him,
but the gods hate sneak attacks as much as we do.
All who slandered Heracles are in Hell now,
and their city's in slavery. Including
these bedraggled women, lost to prosperity
as your husband wished. As he commanded,
so I have done. When he has made his offerings
to Zeus, he will be here with you himself.
Of all my happy news, this must sound best to you.

CHORUS
    O Queen, your happiness is visible, for now,   270
    and for the promised future.

DEIANIRA
    Yes. My husband's success has given me
    every reason to give free rein to joy.
    My happiness deserves no less a range
    than his triumphs. And yet one can't help
    feeling, deep inside, that he who rises
    so high can also be brought low.
    When I beheld these captives, women
    without a homeland, fatherless strangers,
    a grief for them overcame me terribly.   280
    Now they must live as slaves, though earlier
    they may have been the children of free men.

    O Zeus, who turns the tide in men's affairs,
    I pray you will never act so against
    my children, or if you must, not while I live.
    That is my fear, seeing these slaves.
(Deianira questions Iole.)

> You poor girl, who are you? A wife? A mother?
> Clearly this suffering is new to you.
> Are you of noble blood? Whose daughter
> is she, Lichas? Who were her mother and father?   290
> Her face betrays her fate, that's why I pity her most.

LICHAS

> You are asking the wrong person. Maybe
> she isn't the lowliest of her kind.

DEIANIRA

> She's not of royal birth? Did Eurytus have a daughter?

LICHAS

> I haven't questioned her deeply, so don't know.

DEIANIRA

> You haven't heard these women speak her name?

LICHAS

> I've barely spoken to them, so don't know.

DEIANIRA

> Poor girl, tell us your name. You look as though
> it might be our misfortune not to know you.

LICHAS

> She hasn't said a word before now.   300
> I'd be surprised if she opened her mouth
> except to weep about her troubles
> as if they were birth pangs. That's how
> it's been since we left her windy country.
> If she has to suffer in silence, let's forgive her.

DEIANIRA

> I won't trouble her more then, to multiply
> her sadness; it's heavy enough already.

Let her come into the house with us,
then you can leave when you wish, and I
can see to the arrangements inside.   310

*(Deianira begins to lead Lichas and the captives, but as the others enter
the house the Messenger comes forward to speak
to her.)*

MESSENGER

Wait! A word with you alone, without
these others. I know things of these captives
no one has told you, but should have.
I can tell you what you ought to know.

DEIANIRA

Out of my way! What do you want with me?

MESSENGER

Listen to me. What I will tell you now
is more important than all I said before.

DEIANIRA

Is it for my ears only, and my friends,
or should I call the others back as well?

MESSENGER

I will speak to you and these women, not the others.   320

DEIANIRA

The others are inside. What is this story?

MESSENGER

That man has not been telling you the truth.
He's lying, or else he was dishonest before.

DEIANIRA

What are you saying? I don't understand.
Tell me everything, from beginning to end.

MESSENGER

> With my own ears I heard this man say—
> and there were others who'll attest to it—
> that Heracles destroyed Eurytus
> and his fortified Oechalia for the girl.
> Love alone, of all the gods, drove him   330
> to slaughter. Not slavery to Omphale
> in Lydia; not Iphitus' murder.
> But there's no mention of Love in the story
> this man just told you here! When Heracles
> couldn't convince the father to donate
> his daughter for his bedmate, he made up
> a pretty tale to excuse going to war
> against her country, and killed Eurytus,
> her father, then sacked his city. Now,
> on his return, he's sent her on ahead   340
> under protection, hardly as a slave.
> I wouldn't expect that, seeing he's mad for her.
> I thought I'd better reveal the story I heard
> when he told the others in the marketplace
> of Trachis, my lady, where many men were gathered.
> They can attest to all I've said. Forgive me
> if what I've told you hurts, but I have said
> only the complete truth.

DEIANIRA

> O God, What is this now? What trouble
> have I invited under my roof?   350
> A girl so beautiful and well-born,
> and Lichas swore she didn't have a name?

MESSENGER

> Yes, Eurytus was her father. Her name
> is Iole, but Lichas couldn't tell you that,
> because he never asked.

CHORUS
>   The damndest of the damned
>   is the scheming liar.

DEIANIRA
>   What shall I do, friends?
>   I am so shocked I cannot think!
>   Tell me what to do!   360

CHORUS
>   Confront Lichas with the truth,
>   insist that he verify it to you.

DEIANIRA
>   Yes, that's good advice. I will.

MESSENGER
>   What do you wish? Shall I remain here?

DEIANIRA
>   Stay. Here he comes from the house
>   without being summoned.
>   *(Enter Lichas through the house door.)*

LICHAS
>   What message shall I bring to Heracles,
>   my lady? I'm going to him now.

DEIANIRA
>   So long to get here, and now you're hurrying off
>   before we've hardly had a word together?   370

LICHAS
>   What do you wish to know? What can I tell you?

DEIANIRA
Will you tell me the whole truth?

LICHAS
Whatever I know—I swear by Zeus.

DEIANIRA
Who is that girl you brought here?

LICHAS
She's a Euboean. Her parents aren't known to me.

MESSENGER
See here! Who do you think you're talking to?

LICHAS
And you yourself. What do you mean,
questioning me this way?

MESSENGER
You'd be wise to give me an answer.

LICHAS
I'm addressing my mistress Deianira,   380
Heracles' wife, the daughter of Oeneus—
unless my eyes are playing tricks on me.

MESSENGER
That's what I was hoping you'd say.
Your mistress, correct?

LICHAS
No other answer would be true.

MESSENGER
What shall your punishment be then,
if you have been lying to her?

LICHAS

Lying? What kind of trick is this?

MESSENGER

There's only one trick here. The one you're playing.

LICHAS

I'm off. I'm foolish to have listened this long.   390

MESSENGER

Not yet. Not until you answer one straight question.

LICHAS

Ask away. I know you have words enough.

MESSENGER

The captive girl you brought here—
you know the one I mean?

LICHAS

I do. What about her?

MESSENGER

You pretend to know nothing of her,
but didn't you say before that she was Iole,
the daughter of Eurytus?

LICHAS

Where did I say it? Where is the man
who'll swear he heard me say it?   400

MESSENGER

Many townspeople heard you. You said it
to a crowd in the marketplace, at Trachis.

LICHAS

> Oh, sure, that's what they *thought* they heard.
> It's their opinion, not my actual words.

MESSENGER

> Opinion, hah! You swore an oath this girl
> was going to be the bride of Heracles.

LICHAS

> The bride of Heracles? For God's sake,
> Deianira, who is this strange fellow?

MESSENGER

> This fellow heard you say that her city
> was wiped out because of Heracles' desire   410
> for the girl. It had nothing to do with
> the Lydian woman, just passion for the girl.

LICHAS

> Dismiss this fellow, my lady. Sane men
> do not cross words with the insane.

DEIANIRA

> By Zeus whose bolts light Oeta's highest fields,
> don't rob me of an honest answer! Tell me
> the truth and you'll discover that I won't
> hold it against you, that I know
> the fickle hearts of men and how they change.
> Only a fool tries to trade punches with Love,   420
> who pummels even the gods when they contest him.
> He governs me as he does any woman,
> so I'd be mad to blame my husband
> for catching this sickness, let alone that girl.
> She has done nothing wrong, and not harmed me.
> Out of the question. If Heracles taught you to lie,
> you went to a dishonest school, but if
> you taught yourself, you appear only a liar,

not a considerate man, which pains me all the more.
Tell me the truth. It's no honor for a free man   430
to be known everywhere as a liar.
You have spoken to many, and I'll learn
from them, if not from you. Don't be afraid
to hurt me. *Not* knowing hurts me worse.
What's so terrible? Heracles has had
a lot of women, yet I've never besmirched one.
Nor will I insult this one, who may be
demolished by her passion. Didn't I take pity
when I saw her, knowing her beauty
has caused her ruin? Through no act of hers   440
she has wrecked her homeland. All this
is water under the wind's power. But you:
tell lies to others; tell the truth to me.

CHORUS

Take her advice. Obey her, and you'll have
no trouble later. All of us will thank you.

LICHAS

I see that you are practical, dear mistress,
and take things as they are. Here's the truth,
without holding back. As this man said,
Heracles was overcome with desire
for this girl. It was for her he laid waste   450
to her fatherland, Oechalia. Your husband
never denied it, or asked me to disguise
his actions, to be fair to him. It was
I myself, and done, my lady, that I shouldn't
bring you harm. All fault is mine.
Now you know everything, but for your sake
as well as his, take pity on her
as you did before. The strength of Heracles
has always triumphed, but now his passion
has him cornered at spear's point.   460

DEIANIRA

You speak as though you knew my mind.
I won't pile useless struggle with the Gods
on the weight of my afflictions.
Come inside with me. There are messages
to bring to Heracles, and gifts for you
who brought such gifts to me. You must take them.
It wouldn't do to leave with empty hands
when you marched here with such riches.
(They enter the house.)

CHORUS

The power of Goddess Aphrodite
always wins. Forget the gods.   470
Didn't she make a fool
of Zeus, the sky-god, and Hades,
ruler of the Underworld,
and earth-shaking Poseidon?
But who joined in the courtship
struggle for Deianira's hand,
which two stirred the dust
to clouds and stormed each other
with body blows?

One was that high-horned   480
four-footed bull of a river,
Achelous, and the other,
from Thebes of Bacchus,
carried a supple bow,
war club, and spears—
the son of Zeus,
fierce and unconquerable.
They met in the ring, eager
for Deianira's bed,
with Aphrodite, Love's   490
referee, between them.

Fist-smash and twang
of bowstring mingling with
sweep and hook of horns,
confused wrestling,
head-thuds, groaning
from twisted mouths,
while that girl whose eyes
had driven them to this
sat away on a hillside   500
awaiting the victor.
So it went, as I tell you,
chest to chest, arm
against leg, while
a pitiful beauty awaited
the outcome, when she
would be taken like a calf
lost to her mother.

(Deianira comes from the house bearing a small, sealed casket.)

DEIANIRA

Dear women, while our guest speaks
to the captives before he departs,   510
I have slipped out to tell you
what my hands have done, and to ask
your sympathy for all I'm suffering.
Now I have welcomed into my house
a girl—but not a girl, no virgin!—
a piece of damaged goods—as a ship's
captain takes on troublesome cargo.
My heart burns with this insult—
two women waiting for Heracles
under the same sheet! This is the gift   520
my courageous, faithful husband
sends me to reward my constancy
here at home so many years. Still,
I'm not angry. He's been afflicted with

the same sickness so often in the past.
But to share my house and that man
with her, who would stand for it?
Now she is coming into her full flowering
and I am waning. Men's eyes are drawn
to the unplucked blossom; their feet   530
withdraw from the drying stalk.
I fear Heracles will be called
my husband, but he'll be called her man.
As I've said, it makes no sense for a woman
to let her anger have its way with her.
Here's my plan to free myself.

For many years I've kept in a copper urn
the gift a centaur gave me long ago.
As a girl I took blood from the dying
Nessus' wounds, that ancient hairy creature.   540
For a price he'd ferry people across
the Evenus' depths, without oars or sails.
He bore me over on his shoulders the day I left
my father's house as the bride of Heracles.
Halfway across, he felt me lustfully.
I screamed and the son of Zeus, ahead,
turned and sent an arrow
into his lungs. The centaur spoke
his last words to me: "Listen, daughter
of Oeneus, and you'll be rewarded,   550
since you are the last to be ferried by me.
Collect the clots of my blood that are black
with the Lernean Hydra's venomed bile,
in which Heracles dipped his arrows. This charm
will rule your husband's heart; never will he
look at another woman and love her more than you."
Since Nessus died I've kept it in the house, locked away,
and now have need of it. I've done
exactly as the centaur told me. This robe
is smeared with the love-charm. Now we are ready.   560

May I never be the kind of woman who connives
to do evil, for I hate such women.
But if these spells and charms will overcome
that girl and return Heracles to me—
Well, it's done, unless I'm acting recklessly.
Tell me if you think so, and I'll stop.

CHORUS

If you believe in what you've done
we cannot say you have acted rashly.

DEIANIRA

I can only hope. I've taken the chance,
but only the outcome will tell for sure.   570

CHORUS

What happens must be your proof. You have
no way of knowing, otherwise.

DEIANIRA

We'll have the answer soon. Lichas is coming
from the house, soon to be leaving.
Keep our secret. What's done in the dark
may be shameful, but it's not a scandal, at least.
(*Enter Lichas from the house.*)

LICHAS

Oeneus' daughter, I am late in leaving.
What are your instructions for me?

DEIANIRA

Lichas, I have been preparing something
while you were inside talking to the captives.   580
With my own hands I made this robe, a gift
for my husband. Take it to him, but when
you present it tell him no man but he
should touch it or wear it. Not sunlight,

or firelight from a hearth or altar,
should shine on it, until it arrays him
before the gods on a day of bull-offerings.
I vowed that, at his safe homecoming,
in reverence I would enfold him in it
so he appears at sacrifice to the gods   590
dressed in beauty as never before.
Here's my seal upon the casket,
this circle he'll recognize. Go now,
but remember: a messenger should carry
only what he's been told. This way you'll earn
twice the thanks, my husband's and my own.

LICHAS
     If I take my example from Hermes,
     greatest of messengers, I won't
     be tripped up, but present this gift,
     and your words exactly as you've said them.   600

DEIANIRA
     Go, then. You know what to report
     of things here in this house?

LICHAS
     I do. All's well, I'll tell him.

DEIANIRA
     And since you saw how I welcomed that girl,
     you'll say I treated her with friendship?

LICHAS
     Yes, your kindness moved me deeply.

DEIANIRA
     What else? I won't speak yet about
     my love for him; it's too soon for that.
     I'll wait and see if he returns my longing.
     (Exit Lichas. Deianira enters the house.)

CHORUS

    All you who live by harbors,   610
    by hot springs bubbling
    from the rocks, beneath
    the heights of Oeta,
    on the shores of the sea
    of Malis, the coast where
    golden-arrowed Artemis
    protects, and there
    at Thermopylae, where
    Greeks hold their councils,

    soon you'll hear flute-music   620
    floating sweetly among you,
    not rage's dissonance
    but lyre-music fit for
    the ears of gods, fit
    for the son of Zeus
    and Alcmene, who hurries
    home bearing the treasures
    of conquest.

    We waited the twelve months
    he was gone from us, having   630
    no word of him, fearing
    all the sea could do,
    and his constant wife
    wept for him, wept out
    her love, heart-broken.
    But now the war-god Ares,
    like a bull fly-stung
    to madness, has changed
    her fortune.
    O let him come swiftly   640
    in his ship of many oars,
    crossing the ocean swiftly,
    never stopping until he arrives

home from the island altar
where he sacrifices.
Return him, wild with desire,
in the robe anointed
as the centaur advised.
(Deianira comes from the house.)

DEIANIRA
O my friends! Now I am fearful!
Have I gone too far in what I've done?   650

CHORUS
Why are you troubled, Deianira?

DEIANIRA
I don't know, but something tells me disaster
will follow from what I did in all hope.

CHORUS
Do you mean the robe you sent to Heracles?

DEIANIRA
Yes, Yes. No one should act blindly,
when the outcome cannot be foreseen.

CHORUS
Why are you afraid? Tell us if you can.

DEIANIRA
When you hear what has just happened,
you will think it incredible.
When I smeared the ointment on my husband's   660
robe, the clump of sheep's wool I used
vanished away. Nothing in the house
consumed it—as if it ate itself
and crumbled there on the stones.

Here's exactly how it happened,
I want you to know every detail.

I followed to the letter everything
that beastly centaur told me, as he lay
with the death-bearing arrow in his side.
I knew his words like something cut in bronze: 670
I kept the drug from fire, even from
sunlight, always in the dark and untouched,
until it was time to smear it. Then,
when I was ready, in the dark of the house
I smeared it on a piece of wool I'd plucked
from our flocks, and spread it on the robe,
which I folded and put in the casket
you saw, before the sun could touch it.

When I went in again I saw something
I can't understand, or explain to anyone.   680
That clump of wool—somehow without thinking
I must have thrown it into full sunlight.
When it heated, it shriveled and crumbled
into powder, like a drift of sawdust
fallen from new-cut wood. It lay there,
and from the ground a foam boiled up
as if someone had poured out the liquor
of Dionysus' blue-green grapes.
What shall I think? Now I've done something
awful. That monster Nessus! How could I   690
have thought he'd shown me kindness,
since I'd caused his death? He tricked me
to murder the man who'd killed him.
I see it, now that it's too late.
Unless I'm wrong, I'm the unhappy wife
who's going to kill her husband. That arrow
wounded even Chiron, an immortal, and kills
whatever it strikes. The same black poison

oozing from the bloody side of Nessus
will kill Heracles, I know it now!   700
That's what I fear. And I'll die with him,
if it does. My mind's made up. How can I live
and hear my name coupled with disgrace,
when all I intended was for good?

CHORUS

Though all you expect may happen,
hold on to hope until things come to pass.

DEIANIRA

How can I hope for anything when scheming
played its part in all I planned?

CHORUS

No one who knows the story will be angry,
they'll see your innocence and be forgiving.   710

DEIANIRA

Your own innocence is speaking now.
That's easy, since you've done nothing wrong.

CHORUS

Hyllus is here, who went to find his father.
Quiet! Unless you'd have him know.
(Enter Hyllus.)

HYLLUS

Mother! I wish I'd found you dead,
or if not dead then someone else's mother.
Or else, with a better heart than yours inside you.
Of these three wishes, any one would do.

DEIANIRA

My son, what have I done to earn such hatred?

HYLLUS

What have you done? You have murdered   720
your husband and my father.

DEIANIRA

    No, no, my son! What are you saying?

HYLLUS

    Only the truth! Who can change events
    once they have been seen to happen?

DEIANIRA

    What are you saying? Who will attest
    to this terrible act you accuse me of?

HYLLUS

    With these two eyes I saw my father fall!
    It was no rumor anybody brought me.

DEIANIRA

    Where did it happen? You were at his side?

HYLLUS

    If you have to hear, I'll tell you everything.   730
    After he took Eurytus' great city, he left
    with the trophies and first-fruits of conquest.
    At the cape called Cenaeum, at Euboea,
    he marked off altars and a sacred grove
    for Zeus, his father, and there to my happiness
    I saw him. He was about to celebrate
    with an abundant sacrifice when Lichas,
    his herald, arrived from here bearing your gift,
    the death-besotted robe. As you had wished,
    he put it on and killed twelve bulls,   740
    the finest of his plunder, then increased
    the sacrifice to a hundred, slaughtering
    all that were brought to the altar.
    He was at peace, poor man, proud in that robe,
    and offering his prayers to the gods.
    Then, as the flames leaped, feeding on
    pinewood sap and the sacrificial blood,

he began to sweat, and the robe clung to him
everywhere, tight as a second skin painted
on him. Pain gnawed him to his bones,   750
convulsed him into spasms, as though
a vicious serpent's poison ate his flesh.
Then he cried out against poor Lichas,
blaming him for your evil act, demanding
to know what plot that robe had set afoot.
Lichas, who knew nothing, could only say
the gift was yours alone, delivered
as you had bid him. As Heracles heard,
a torment squeezed his lungs. He grabbed
Lichas by the ankle and dashed him against   760
a rock the sea broke over, smashing his skull,
red blood and white brain-matter
mingling in his hair. All who saw cried out,
for the dead man, and for the man engaged
with pain in his own death-struggle; but no one
would approach my screaming father, who fell
and leaped then fell again, tossing with agony
while the rocks echoed with his howling
from Locris' mountains to Euboea's cliffs.
Exhausted at last, worn out with crying   770
and crawling in the dust and lamenting
his execrable marriage to you, and all
he had endured to win you from Oeneus, only
to come to this, he lifted his head,
eyes rolling like a beast's, out of the smoke
that hung about him, and saw me weeping
among the onlookers. He called to me:
"My son, come here! Do not deny me
in my misery. Come here, though it mean
you may die with me. Take me away from here.   780
Some place where no man will set eyes on me.
Pity me enough to take me from this land,
at least, and quickly. Don't let me die here!"

So he commanded. We brought him carefully
onto a ship and landed him on this shore,
hard going, while he lay bellowing.
You'll see him soon, alive or dead just now.

Mother, you've done these things you planned
and now you're caught! Justice will punish you,
and the Furies will take revenge! Thus   790
I curse you, if it is a son's right. And it is,
for you gave me the right when you murdered
the best of men. His like shall not be seen again.
(Deianira goes toward the house.)

CHORUS
Why do you leave quietly? Don't you know
your silence pleads your accuser's case?
(Deianira enters the house.)

HYLLUS
Let her go. May a fair wind carry her
from my sight. Why should she be called "Mother,"
who's so unmotherly? Let her go.
Good riddance. May the happiness she brought
my father be hers as well.   800
(Exit Hyllus off stage.)

CHORUS
O women, suddenly that prophecy
spoken so long ago has come to pass:
when the year of the twelfth plowing
was ended, it foretold, the son of Zeus
would be delivered from his labors.
Now it comes home as promised,
like a ship crossing mild seas.
When a man is dead, how can he have labors?

If the centaur's treacherous poison
clings to him in a murderous cloud—   810
death's poison nurtured by
the shimmering serpent, and soaking
into his sides, the monstrous
Hydra's essence soaking in—
how shall he see tomorrow's sun?
Now the black-maned centaur's words
are arrows burning him with their treachery.
Poor Deianira knew nothing of this,
but saw only the destruction
of her marriage by a young wife   820
newly arrived in her house,
and acted to save her family.
She knew nothing of the centaur's
vile contrivance, learned only
in the accident of their unfortunate
meeting, and now she weeps out
her broken heart as doom draws nearer
to reveal the perfidious finality.

Tears like a waterfall!
Heracles suffers such pitiful   830
illness as no enemy ever inflicted on him.
Alas for the victorious spear-head
that won him this lethal bride
from Oechalia's mountains.
But we know whose hand stirs
these events: it is the work
of Cyprian Aphrodite, the silent one.
(Wailing within the house.)

CHORUS *(spoken alternately)*
What's this? Is someone inside the house
crying out in their grief?

What can it be but that? Only deeper suffering   840
could be the cause of so much weeping.
(Nurse enters from the house.)
    And now the nurse is coming to tell us something.
    How sad she looks, the poor old woman.

NURSE

    O women, the robe she sent to Heracles.
    It's only begun to cause us endless sorrow.

CHORUS

    Tell us, woman. What new calamity's in there?

NURSE

    Without taking a step, Deianira's
    begun her final journey.

CHORUS

    She's dead, then?

NURSE

    Nothing else to say.   850

CHORUS

    The poor woman is dead?

NURSE

    I'll say it again, Deianira is dead.

CHORUS

    The poor thing. How did she die?

NURSE

    Awful. Terrible.

CHORUS
> But how, tell us how.

NURSE
> By her own hand.

CHORUS
> In rage? In madness?

NURSE
> On a weapon's point.

CHORUS
> One death on another?
> And she died alone?   860

NURSE
> Cold sharp steel.

CHORUS
> You saw it? You were there?

NURSE
> I was beside her. Yes, I saw.

CHORUS
> How? How did it happen? Speak?

NURSE
> By herself. Her own hand did it.

CHORUS
> What are you telling us?

NURSE
> Only the truth.

CHORUS

That young bride, just arrived!
Already she's given birth
to a huge wrath in this house.   870

NURSE

It's true, and had you seen that wrath
you'd be weeping more than you are.

CHORUS

How could a woman's hands bring this about?

NURSE

They could, as I will tell you. Don't judge
until you've heard everything. She went
into the house and saw Hyllus
preparing a soft litter in the courtyard
to bring back to his father. She hid
herself away and knelt before the altars,
bawling that henceforth they'd be alone.   880
Whenever she touched a familiar
household object, she'd weep. Poor thing!
She wandered weeping through the house,
back and forth, with no design, and when
she saw a servant she loved, she'd cry
again, lamenting her fate aloud, and the
future of her house empty of children.
Suddenly she stopped, and rushed into
the bedroom she had shared with Heracles.
I watched her from the shadows. Making   890
their bed, she threw herself into it
and sat there—her marriage bed—
and spoke to it through a rush of hot tears:
"Goodbye forever, my bed, sweet bridal chamber.
You'll never hold me as a wife again."
Only that, and violently swept her arm

to a gold pin holding her robe, and bared
her left side. I ran with all my strength
to tell her son, but before we returned she'd done it:
opened her side, entrails and heart,   900
with a two-edged sword. Hyllus
cried out that his rage had driven her to this;
others in the house had just told him
of her mistake, how the centaur tricked her.
The poor boy gave himself up to grief.

He pressed his living heart to hers and kissed
her lips, crying that he'd stabbed her
with slander, bemoaning his doubled loss,
twice orphaned of mother and father in a day.
Learn from what has happened in this house.   910
Whoever depends on tomorrow or the next day
is a fool! Tomorrow is nothing until
we have passed today without harm.
(Nurse enters the house.)

CHORUS
In my sorrow I cannot say
which death I should lament first,
the one in the house, or the one
I await, that is coming here.
Or is it all one?

I wish a strong wind
would take me away from here   920
so I won't die of fright
merely for laying eyes on
the brave son of Zeus,
borne here in an agony
without a cure. Who
could imagine such a thing?
*(Enter Heracles, on a litter borne by servants, with an old man. Enter
Hyllus from the house.)*

He is nearer now, whom I cried for
like a sorrowing bird in the night.
Strangers are coming, silent, slow,
like men on a death march, silent.   930
Is he dead or alive? Or only sleeping?

HYLLUS

Father? Tell me what to do.
How can I help? Don't leave
me here, alone and grieving.

OLD MAN

Quiet, my boy. Don't aggravate
his pain, lest he become savage
again. He's down, but he's alive.
Hold your tongue.

HYLLUS

Is he truly alive?

OLD MAN

He's sleeping deeply now.   940
Don't get him worked up.
It only enrages his sickness,
which is dormant for now.

HYLLUS

The weight of his condition
sits on me. There's nothing
I can do, and it drives me mad.

HERACLES

O Zeus, where am I? What men
are these, watching me
beaten down with this affliction?
The pain! The teeth!   950
That monster's teeth!

OLD MAN

> See what you've done?
> I told you to be quiet
> and let the sleep remain
> in his head and on his eyes.

HYLLUS

> I couldn't bear his agony in silence.

HERACLES

> Is this the thanks I get,
> O altar at Cenaeum, for all
> my sacrifices on your stones?
> O Zeus, all you give me   960
> is torment. I wish these
> accursed eyes had never seen you.
> And now they have to watch
> madness unfold in me
> like some inevitable flower.
> What cure is there for this?
> What spell-singer or miracle
> can drive this from me? Only Zeus?

(The old man tries to help.)

> Leave me alone! Let me sleep
> a deep and final sleep,   970
> away from pain. Don't touch me!
> What are you doing?
> You're killing me! You woke
> the slumbering agony again.

> Here it comes. I'm caught!
> Greeks! Ingrates! I wrecked my life
> ridding the seas and woods
> of threatening beasts, and now
> not one of you will give me rest.
> Who'll give me the merciful   980

sword, the welcome fire?
Won't one of you
separate this head
from this despicable body?

OLD MAN

Come, you're his son, and stronger
than I. Help me to make him comfortable.

HYLLUS

I can hold him, but I can't cure him,
nor can any man. This is Zeus' doing.

HERACLES

Where are you, Hyllus. Help me,
my son. Raise me up. Ow! Ow!   990
What's happening to me?

That evil thing! It lunges,
devouring me again. No cure
against its savagery.
O Pallas, what pain! Have mercy
on your father, my son. Put me
to the sword, no one will blame you.
Stab my heart! Kill the agony
your evil mother caused. I wish
my torments were hers, revenge   1000
for her perfidious ways.

Sweet Hades, brother of Zeus,
put me to sleep, end this quickly,
give me my doom.

CHORUS

Oh friends, this great king's tragedy—
driven mad with suffering.

HERACLES

Even to speak of the legendary
labors of these hands and this back
hurts me now, for nothing the wife of Zeus
or that cruel master Eurystheus   1010
did to me equals this torment
that doublefaced daughter of Oeneus
has woven into my flesh, this net
devised by Furies. It devours me.
It's alive, and sucks my breath
out of my lungs. It has drunk my blood
and left me a cadaver in its clutches.
No spear, no swarm of earth-born giants,
no savage beast, no man of Greece
or of a barbarous tongue, not even   1020
all the lands I scoured of evils
together could accomplish this. Only a woman,
a warrior's opposite without a weapon,
has laid me low, my son.

If you are truly my son, don't honor
your mother's name more than mine.
Bring her to me with your own hands
and put her into mine, she who gave you life.
Let's see what hurts you most, my twisted
body, or hers when I am through with it,   1030
when I have given her what she deserves.
Show courage, my son, and do as I say.
Pity me as any stranger would, for never
has anyone seen me like this, weeping
and carrying on like some girl.
Even in my most dreaded endeavors
I never uttered a fearful word, and now
in this mess I'm exposed as a woman.

Come closer, stand beside me and take
a good look at what's happened to me.   1040

Throw off the covers and look. Look,
everyone! See this miserable body?
See what the wreckage of a hero is?

Ow! Ow! That fire. It's burning me,
shooting through me. It contorts me.
It won't leave me alone. It's eating me.
Receive me, you king of Hell!
Strike me dead, Zeus! Give my head
your thunderbolt! It's devouring me,
blooming in me, strengthening on my flesh.   1050
O you hands, this back and chest.
You withering arms. Was it you who overcame
the elusive Nemean lion, whose fierceness
made shepherds tremble, and the Lernean Hydra,
and the rampant herd of man-horses, monstrous,
powerful, and lawless? And the boar
of Erymanthus, and that three-headed hellhound,
gruesome Echidna's hideous offspring?
Was it you who overcame the dragon protecting
the golden apples at the end of the earth,   1060
my hands, and performed ten thousand other labors,
and let no one beat me ever? And now
I'm wreckage. Something I cannot even see
to grapple with has ripped me, mangled me.
Me, born of the noblest mother, son of Zeus,
the king of Heaven! But hear me out:
even if I'm the lowliest thing there is,
a nothing, incapable even of crawling,
bring me the woman who set this afoot
and my hands will give her a lesson   1070
she can teach the world: Heracles lived
to punish evil, and died punishing it too.

CHORUS
O Greece, if this man dies
your mourning will be endless.

HYLLUS

Father, allow me silence while I tell you
what you have to know. I know you're ill,
but hear me without the wrath that makes you sicker,
or else you won't understand how revenge
and acrimony are impossible here.

HERACLES

Say whatever you want. No riddles.   1080
I hurt too much to unravel them just now.

HYLLUS

It's about my mother. About her mistake
and her condition.

HERACLES

Damn you! You speak of the mother who murdered
your father? And to his dying face?

HYLLUS

Silence is not the remedy for her condition.

HERACLES

You speak the truth, her crimes should be announced.

HYLLUS

What she has done today needs telling, too.

HERACLES

Out with it, then. But don't betray me.

HYLLUS

Here: she's dead. She's just been murdered.   1090

HERACLES

Who did it? This news is too good,
and yet too bad!

HYLLUS

    She did it herself, and she alone.

HERACLES

    I would have done it for her, had she waited.

HYLLUS

    If you knew what you were saying
    you'd quell your rage.

HERACLES

    Go on, finish the story.

HYLLUS

    What she had done as good turned wrong on her.

HERACLES

    You call murdering your father "good"?

HYLLUS

    When she saw your young bride in her house   1100
    she tried to work a love-charm on you.

HERACLES

    In Trachis? Who is there here
    who knows such powerful medicines?

HYLLUS

    Nessus the centaur. He advised her
    to arouse your love with the drug.

HERACLES

    Now I'm dead! I'm dead! It's ended!
    The light goes out, and doom falls!
    Son, you have no more father.
    Call your brothers, and Alcmene, my mother.

Zeus loved her, and she paid for it.   1110
My last words will be the prophecies
That oracles have made about my life.

HYLLUS

Your mother is living by the sea, at Tiryns,
with some of your children, and others
are at Thebes. We who are here
will do whatever you require of us.

HERACLES

Hear me, then. It's time for you to show
what there is of Heracles in you.

My father told me long ago that nothing
alive could kill me, only some dweller   1120
in Hell. It's come true: that centaur
murdered me with his own death, as Zeus
foretold. His words are sustained
by newer prophecies. Listen: here's
what I heard when I went among the Selli
who sleep on the ground. In their mountain
grove I wrote down what my father's oak
said. It speaks in many tongues, and said
that in this present time I'd be set free
from all my labors, which I thought   1130
meant happiness for me. Now I know
it means I'm going to die. Only the dead
are free from toil, my son, it's all
perfectly clear now. Prepare to stand
with me in this last battle. Don't falter
and inflame my wrath, agree freely
to aid me. Obey your father, honor
the highest of all laws.

HYLLUS

O Father, I'm afraid of what you'll say next,
but whatever you want I'll carry it out.   1140

HERACLES
First, give me your right hand.

HYLLUS
Why must I take an oath?

HERACLES
Don't ask. Do as I say.

HYLLUS
Here's my hand, I won't deny you.

HERACLES
Swear by the head of Zeus who fathered me.

HYLLUS
Tell me what I am swearing to.

HERACLES
Swear you will do what I ask, all of it.

HYLLUS
I swear it by the head of Zeus.

HERACLES
Pray for retribution, if you break your oath.

HYLLUS
So I pray, nor will I violate my oath.   1150

HERACLES
The summit of Mount Oeta, sacred to Zeus—
you know it?

HYLLUS
I do. I've sacrificed there often.

HERACLES

> Carry me up there with your own
> hands and the help of any friends you need.
> Then cut down the strongest oaks
> and healthy wild olive trees
> and lay me on them. Kindle the pyre
> with a flaming pine torch. No weeping,
> no crying out! Be your father's son,   1160
> or else I'll be waiting in the next world
> to curse you forever.

HYLLUS

> What? What are you making me do?

HERACLES

> You have to do it or be another man's son.
> If you don't, go find another father.

HYLLUS

> How can you ask it, Father. Your son
> your murderer, polluted with your blood?

HERACLES

> Not murderer, but *healer,*
> the only physician who can cure this pain.

HYLLUS

> I'd cure you by setting fire to you?   1170

HERACLES

> If you're afraid to do it, do the rest.

HYLLUS

> I'll carry you there, at least I can do that.

HERACLES

> And build my pyre the way I asked?

HYLLUS

    I'll have it done, but I won't touch it.
    Trust me in everything else.

HERACLES

    That will be more than enough.
    But one small favor more.

HYLLUS

    Whatever it is, I'll do it.

HERACLES

    You know the girl, Eurytus' daughter?

HYLLUS

    You mean Iole?   1180

HERACLES

    That's her. What I want is this, my son.
    When I'm dead, if you want to be obedient
    to all you've sworn me, you must marry her.
    No man but you should have her, since
    she has slept beside me. Marry her.
    You've obeyed me in these larger things,
    don't lose my thanks over a lesser one.

HYLLUS

    How can I argue with him in his pain?
    But how can I hear this and hold my tongue?

HERACLES

    Are you saying you won't do it?   1190

HYLLUS

    How could I? The girl's responsible
    for my mother's death and your condition.

How could anyone? He'd have to be insane,
his mind alive with the avenging fiends.
Better to burn with you than live
with her, my greatest enemy.

HERACLES

Though I'm dying, you won't do what I ask?
You'll answer to the Gods for it.

HYLLUS

Your sickness is driving you to this.

HERACLES

My sickness was asleep till you provoked it!   1200

HYLLUS

Every way I turn the answer's wrong.

HERACLES

Obey your father and the answer's clear.

HYLLUS

What if obedience means impiety?

HERACLES

To give me joy is no impiety.

HYLLUS

Is this your order? Will you forgive me for it?

HERACLES

Let the Gods be witness to it.

HYLLUS

    Since you've called on the Gods
    to verify your wishes, I'll obey.
    No one can say it's wrong to honor a father.

HERACLES

    You are my son at last. Let your words   1210
    turn quickly to acts of mercy. Put me
    on the pyre before the devouring
    begins in me again. Quickly. Lift me up.
    This is the end, the only rest from toil.

HYLLUS

    Nothing can prevent the completion of all
    you have commanded your son, Father.

HERACLES

    Before the pain awakens entirely,
    let us depart, O my strong soul;
    put a steel bit between my teeth,
    make them like stone to thwart   1220
    my screams until we end this last
    unwanted labor, welcomed now.
(The servants raise the litter and prepare to exit.)

HYLLUS

    Lift him up. And forgive me now
    for what I have to do. You have seen
    how little forgiveness the Gods show
    in everything that's happened here.
    We call them our fathers,
    yet they look upon our suffering
    with open eyes. The future
    is closed to us, but what's here now   1230
    evokes our pity and shames them,

and is hardest of all for this man
in whom the struggle was worked out.
(turns to the leader of the Chorus)
    Woman, leave this house.
    You have seen strange things,
    suffering, and a death beyond imagining,
    and there is nothing here
    that is not Zeus.
(Exeunt all.)

Electra

Translated by
Henry Taylor

Translator's Preface

Electra is a profoundly bitter play, but its bitterness is oddly miti-
gated by its craft, which combines epic and lyric language, intensely emotional moments of delusion and recognition, and scarifying dramatic irony.
At its center is a powerful narrative of an exciting and fatal chariot race—a
race that has not been held, but rather invented and embellished to deceive
listeners. Deception and self-deception are fundamental to *Electra*; less famously but more bleakly than *King Oedipus*, it portrays the march to doom
of those who persist in wrongs they can admit but cannot give up.

Many generations of curses lie in the background of the myth of Electra
and Orestes. The oldest of those invoked in Sophocles' play is the one pro-
nounced by Myrtilus on the house of Pelops, the son of Tantalus who had
come to be king of the Peloponnese—the land to which he gave his own
name. Pelops had won his bride Hippodamia, daughter of Oenomaus, by
treachery and deceit. Oenomaus had decreed that any suitor of Hippodamia
must submit to a chariot race in which the loser would give up his life.
Oenomaus had dispatched twelve or thirteen suitors in this way when
Pelops came along and bribed Myrtilus, the charioteer of Oenomaus, to
sabotage the king's chariot. His reward would be to spend the bridal night
with Hippodamia. The race went off, Oenomaus' chariot wrecked and killed
him, and when Myrtilus attempted to claim his reward, Pelops killed him—
but not so instantly that Myrtilus could not pronounce a curse on Pelops'
descendants.

Among the sons of Pelops and Hippodamia were Atreus and Thyestes,
rivals for the throne of Mycenae. By a series of betrayals each of them briefly
claimed the throne, but Atreus finally succeeded in holding it. He discovered, meanwhile, that Thyestes had ravished his wife, and he harbored his
rage. At last he lured Thyestes back from exile to Mycenae, and served him
a banquet consisting of morsels of his children. Thyestes fell back from the
table and vomited, and put an everlasting curse on the seed of Atreus.

Agamemnon and Menelaus were sons of Atreus; in a battle with Tantalus of Pisa, Agamemnon killed him and claimed his widow Clytemnestra for his unwilling bride; Menelaus later married her sister Helen. Clytemnestra bore Orestes and three or four daughters, including Electra, Iphigenia, and Chrysothemis. When Helen went to Troy with Paris, Agamemnon agreed to join Menelaus in an expedition to punish the Trojans and bring her back; but he owed an old debt to Artemis, whom he had blasphemed during a hunt. She held the Greek fleet at Aulis, by means of either calm or unfavorable winds, until Agamemnon sacrificed Iphigenia.

When the Greeks took Troy and started home, Agamemnon lit a fire at an appointed spot, and a sequence of signal-fires proceeded from there to Mycenae, where Clytemnestra was waiting to take her revenge for her daughter's sacrificial death. She and her lover Aegisthus killed Agamemnon when he returned, and he put a curse on them as he died. Orestes, an exile, and Electra, a virtual prisoner of Clytemnestra and Aegisthus, at last managed to kill Clytemnestra and Aegisthus. In versions other than Sophocles', Orestes is pursued by Furies and at last absolved of his matricidal guilt; this play, however, ends with the deaths of Clytemnestra and Aegisthus and a final statement by the Chorus that the house of Atreus has at last been liberated by an act of completion. Some readers have taken this declaration at face value.

Aeschylus and Euripides had both treated the story of Electra before Sophocles. The *Oresteia* had been performed in 458, and it is now generally agreed that Euripides' *Electra* preceded Sophocles' by about five years, the one having been performed in 418 and the other in 413. Aeschylus and Euripides had each in his way drawn out portrayals of the maddening guilt Orestes suffered following the murder. That Sophocles does not do so has given rise to the notion that he approved of the murders of Clytemnestra and Aegisthus. But Electra, powerfully moving as she sometimes may be, is hard to see as a vehicle for Sophocles' approval of revenge.

The two opening speeches introduce Orestes' goal and its dubious morality. In his first response to the Paedagogus, Orestes says that the advice he sought from the oracle was how to avenge his father's murder. The question whether he should do this is not addressed, but the oracle advises stealth rather than more traditionally heroic behavior.

Electra is heard before she is seen, and as soon as she is visible she enters into an exchange with the Chorus that constitutes the longest lyric passage in the extant plays of Sophocles. The pitch of her emotion does not conceal the steadiness with which she views her situation. One view of her is that she enters the action as a person in a rage for vengeance and leaves it thus, having learned nothing and changed little. During the opening *kommos* she promises to keep her voice raised, and admits that she is incurably outrageous. It may be that her speech and behavior are tinged with madness after the recognition scene. Still, between the opening outcry and the final scene, the emotional torture she undergoes is recognizable and deeply moving. At the end of the play, however, she remarks with chilling sarcasm on Clytemnestra's cries of terror and anguish.

The play begins and ends, then, with attention to an offstage voice; as Ann G. Batchelder (see Bibliography below) has suggested, voice and speech, and the power of words to influence action, are central to this play (42). It pivots on the long and quite fictional account of Orestes' death in a chariot race which, though it never took place, is presented with remarkable immediacy and detail. Rachel Kitzinger (see Bibliography) has made an elegant reading of the Paedagogus' false report and its effects, including the strange emotional ambivalence of Electra's outburst over the putative funeral urn, and her loss of authority: when she acts or speaks on the basis of her belief that Orestes is dead, the audience can see that she is on shaky ground.

When Chrysothemis makes her first entrance, she asks Electra what she is about to say, not what she is about to do; as they argue, Electra accuses Chrysothemis of weakness and opportunism, and says that her declared hatred of Clytemnestra consists only of words, not actions. The emotional force of Electra's anguish moves the Chorus and Chrysothemis toward Electra's view of things by the time of Chrysothemis' first exit.

The next argument is that between Electra and Clytemnestra, during which each woman says something transparently self-damning. In her first speech, Clytemnestra indicates her belief that one human life may have more value than another, when she wonders why Iphigenia was sacrificed instead of one of Menelaus' children. In her longer response, Electra urges Clytemnestra to take care in saying what right she had to kill Agamemnon:

> Be careful that you don't invoke
> some law that calls you to fatal account:
> a law that says we take a life for a life
> would put you next in line for final justice. (572–75)

Whether Electra notices the extent to which her words apply to her own case is a question about which critics disagree. However, her declared intention to pursue a course whose dangers she can see, and the powerful energy of her hatred for Clytemnestra, suggest that she would move willingly toward her own encounter with "final justice." As she says to Chrysothemis during their second encounter, "I envy your discretion and despise your cowardice" (989). It is during this exchange, however, that Electra speaks so vigorously on the basis of information we know to be false. Yet she convinces Chrysothemis, whose information that Orestes lives is correct. So Chrysothemis' decision not to join with Electra in the murder of Aegisthus seems less cowardly and more prudent than the words between them would indicate.

At last, when Electra is convinced that she is in the presence of Orestes, she says, "Oh voice, are you here?" (1184). In the ensuing dialogue, Electra rejoices in her freedom to speak her feelings, while Orestes, single-minded and somewhat limited in his emotional responses, fears that the sound of her joy could cause him harm.

When Aegisthus arrives, the Chorus advise Electra to speak "a few kind words/to him" (1391–92) to allay any suspicions he may have. Then Aegisthus asks questions tangled in attributions of hearsay:

> Which of you knows where the men from Phocis are,
> who came here, they say, with word that Orestes
> has been killed in a chariot-racing accident?
> You: yes, I ask you, who used to be so bold . . . (1394–97)

Aegisthus recognizes his predicament when Orestes suggests that he has been talking to a dead man (1429–30), and asks permission to speak a final word. Electra forbids this, in contrast to her arguments with Clytemnestra, and adds that Aegisthus should not receive burial. This shocking departure from custom (also important in, for example, *Antigone* and *The Children of*

Heracles) occurs in Electra's final speech; there is no retreat from this extremity, which hovers menacingly as the play comes rapidly to a close.

Voice and action constitute one of the dualities that have often been said to be in productive conflict in the play; another consists of good and expediency, which are argued in various ways by Orestes and Electra in dialogue with the Paedagogus and Chrysothemis respectively. The play seems strikingly bitter in its recognition that people are easily swayed from right action by considerations of *kerdos*—profit or advantage. That is the word Orestes uses when he asks what could be wrong with faking his death if something good—advantageous—comes of it. This opposition occurs, too, in the two prayers directly addressed to Apollo—one by Clytemnestra (627–45) and one by Electra (1330–37). Both prayers are selfish requests that things go as the petitioner would have them go.

Another significant opposition arises between the concepts of mind and hand. Of Sophocles' plays, only *Ajax* makes more frequent use of *cheiros* (hand) and words derived from it. Explicit references to things done by hand begin with Orestes' report of the oracle (37) and include the murders of Agamemnon, Clytemnestra, and Aegisthus; the bearing of sacrifices and the urn; the upbringing and surrender to safety of Orestes; the menacing approach of Justice; the cruelty of Clytemnestra's parenthood; and Aegisthus' administration of the kingdom. Explicit references to qualities rooted in *phren-*, *phron-*, and *soph-*, including thought, wisdom, good sense, and the lack thereof, occur in connection with Electra's obduracy as compared to Chrysothemis' prudence, the mind of Agamemnon's ghost beside the Acheron, and the perceptions of Electra and Chrysothemis concerning the latter's discovery of libations at Agamemnon's tomb. Two striking examples are in the Paedagogus' interruption of the reunion between Orestes and Electra, in which he is quite plainly out of patience with their foolishness and anxious that they go into action, and in the Chorus' second stasimon, the ode that begins with praise of the wisdom of birds, and calls on the ghost of Agamemnon to help his children. In the end, it is the hand, unencumbered by just or prudent thinking, that completes the action.

A few notes on production: Mute characters of some importance constitute a challenge regularly encountered in Greek tragedy. The audiences of the play's earliest productions would have known that Orestes and Pylades became fast friends during Orestes' exile, and that one version of the legend has Pylades married to Electra after the deaths of Clytemnestra and Aegisthus. For such an audience Pylades' presence in the play would have evoked valuable associations of friendship and loyalty. Nevertheless, a director might be excused for wanting to get rid of him, and even for doing so.

A second issue of direction concerns the Chorus. In most productions in our time, it makes sense to have choral passages delivered in the most plausible manner available. Some translators—myself included, on an earlier occasion—make their own decisions about when to have the chorus represented by its leader, when to have the chorus speak in unison, and when to divide choral passages into short speeches for individual choristers. In this instance, the difficulties of the opening exchange between the Chorus and Electra are obtrusive, and how they are approached is bound to be strongly determined by the abilities of the cast. The play attains nearly to operatic intensity at such moments—another is Electra's surge into lyricism near the end of her speech over the urn—and performers should strive with them within their capabilities.

Finally, though the word "Paedagogus" is not spoken during the play, it will appear in a program. To render it as "Old Slave" or "Tutor" seems adequate in many ways, but I have preferred to have the echoes of words derived from it. It should be clear, though, that it is a common noun, not a person's name.

BIBLIOGRAPHY

The items listed below are those on which I depended so heavily that the translation would have been quite different if any of them had escaped my notice. Over the years I have of course encountered other versions of the play, and consulted as well Robert Graves's *The Greek Myths* and Carolyne Larrington's *The Feminist Companion to Mythology*. Where editors disagree concerning the text, I have generally followed J. H. Kells; a few exceptions are noted below. Ann G. Batchelder and Rachel Kitzinger, though they disagree on some points, have given me invaluable ways of thinking about the words in the play. And every time I log on, I wonder all over again at the splendid usefulness of the Perseus Project.

Ann G. Batchelder. *The Seal of Orestes: Self-Reference and Authority in Soph-ocles' Electra*. Lanham, Md.: Rowman and Littlefield Publishers, 1995.

Gregory Crane, editor-in-chief. The Perseus Project. An Evolving Digital Library. http://www.perseus.tufts.edu.

J. H. Kells, ed. *Sophocles: Electra*. Cambridge: Cambridge University Press, 1973.

Rachel Kitzinger. "Why Mourning Becomes Elektra." *Classical Antiquity* 10, 2 (October 1991): 298–327.

Hugh Lloyd-Jones, ed. and trans. *Sophocles: Ajax / Electra / Oedipus Tyran-nus*. Cambridge, Mass.: Harvard University Press / Loeb Classical Library, 1994.

Hugh Lloyd-Jones and N. G. Wilson, eds. *Sophoclis Fabulae*. Oxford: Oxford University Press, 1990.

————. *Sophoclea: Studies in the Text of Sophocles*. Oxford: Oxford University Press, 1990.

ANNOTATIONS

The first line number refers to the translation; the second, in square brackets, refers to the Greek.

6 [5]. Io is prominent in the choral ode of A. E. Housman's great parody, "Fragment of a Greek Tragedy"; the language there—"the Inachean daugh-ter, loved of Zeus"—is unnervingly close to the literal meaning of this line: "the gadfly-tormented daughter of Inachus."

8 [7]. Apollo the wolf-killer. Literally, "the Lycian god, killer of wolves." Kells notes that the origin of this epithet for Apollo is obscure; "Lycian" occurs again at [645] and 1333 [1379].

33–34 [32–33]. Kells, citing J. T. Sheppard, argues persuasively for the sig-nificance of Orestes' inquiry of Pythia, the Delphic oracle. He asked not whether but how he should kill his mother, thereby forestalling any preven-tive advice.

45–46 [45]. Phanoteus of Phocis "is said to have fought in the womb with his brother Crisus. Crisus was the brother of Strophius, the father of Orestes' friend Pylades, who lodged and entertained Orestes in exile. Since Phanoteus was thus at hereditary feud with Strophius, it was plausible to represent Phanoteus as the friend of Aegisthus and Clytemnestra who sends them advance news of Orestes' death, and Strophius as the one who actually tends Orestes' supposed remains, and sends them home for burial" (Kells 83–84).

47 [47]. Fill in the details. Editors disagree whether the Greek indicates "tell them, swearing to it" or "tell them, filling it out." Kells prefers the latter, Lloyd-Jones and Wilson the former.

48 [49]. Pythian games. Batchelder notes that "Orestes' choice of the Pythian games is an anachronism" previously pointed out by scholia and much more recent critics. "The Pythian games," she writes, "were originally not contests of athletics, but contests of music and poetry celebrated in honor of Apollo. Even after athletic contests were introduced, μουσικοι ('musical and poetic') contests were still the first of the day. They were then followed by the athletic contests in the order in which the Paedagogus will present them" (93–94). Batchelder is persuasive that, despite general agreement that this anachronism is insignificant, it works subtly but powerfully to create the kind of dramatic irony for which Sophocles is particularly well known: the Paedagogus is telling a fictional tale of Orestes' death and providing the audience, who recognize the fiction for what it is, with a true tale of Orestes' present entry into a contest of dramatic production.

103–4 [107]; see also 144 [148]. The nightingale that kills her children is Procne, sister of Philomela and mother of Itys.

107–11 [110–12]. Electra here calls on the rulers of the Underworld, Hades and Persephone; then on Hermes, who guided souls to the realm of Hades; then on the curse Agamemnon is supposed to have called down on his killers; then on the Erinyes, the Furies, who pursued and maddened those who had committed certain crimes—such as Orestes the matricide, in Aeschylus' version of the story.

151 [158]. Iphianassa. "She was a mere name which Sophocles found in his epic sources (cf. *Iliad* 9.145: Agamemnon's daughters Chrysothemis,

Laodice and Iphianassa), used here to pad out a verse, and could afterwards discard. Such was the non-realistic character of this kind of drama" (Kells 92).

479–81 [489–91]. "The avenging Fury is often conceived as a monster who *stalks* her prey, like a wild animal" (Kells 119).

493ff. [500ff.]. The cheating ride of Pelops: see p. 129.

552–53. The Greek is far from clear as to the relation between the winds and the ships at Aulis; the ships were detained either by calm or by unfavorable winds (Kells 126).

634 [645] and 643 [655]. Apollo of the Light: see note to line 8.

685ff. The nationalities of the charioteers are contemporaneous with Sophocles. The name of Orestes is not explicit in connection with the fifth contestant, who is referred to as "he the aforesaid." It seemed finally too clever to write "our hero" here, but the temptation was strong.

769–70 [792–93]. Electra calls on Nemesis, the nymph-goddess of divine vengeance.

810 [837]. "Amphiaraus died betrayed by his wife Eriphyle, who had been bribed with a golden necklace; their son Alcmaeon later avenged his father by killing his mother" (Lloyd-Jones 241). The death of Eriphyle at Alcmeon's hands is the main subject of Housman's "Fragment of a Greek Tragedy."

814 [841]. *Pampsychos* is unique, and has been translated either "with many souls around him" or "full-souled among the lost" (Kells 157). Kells prefers the former; I adopt the reading of Jebb and others.

1020–57 [1058–97], second stasimon. Kells (178–81) is unusually detailed in his commentary on this ode, which I have translated in accordance with his reading, as I understand it. It has sometimes been read as a criticism of Chrysothemis' reluctance, but Kells is persuasive that it asks Agamemnon's ghost to come to his children's aid.

1026 [1064]. Themis: here, a nymph-goddess associated with order, rather than the Titan mother of the Fates and Hours.

1219 [1264]. And with their help had done what I have done: I have invented this line, which is missing from the Greek.

1380–84 [1427–30]. Though these lines make sense as they stand, the metrical evidence is that four lines are missing from this passage: after 1381, two lines of Orestes' and one of Electra's; then after 1383, one of Orestes' (Kells 221; Lloyd-Jones 309).

Cast

THE PAEDAGOGUS, old mentor of Orestes
ORESTES, brother of Electra
ELECTRA, daughter of Agamemnon and Clytemnestra
CHORUS of Argive women
CHRYSOTHEMIS, sister of Electra and Orestes
CLYTEMNESTRA, mother of Electra, Orestes, and Chrysothemis
AEGISTHUS, husband of Clytemnestra
NONSPEAKING
    Pylades, friend of Orestes
    Attendants

*(The scene is before the palace at Mycenae; the time is a couple
    of decades after the Trojan War. A statue of Apollo stands to one
    side of the palace doors. Enter Orestes, Pylades, and the
    Paedagogus.)*

PAEDAGOGUS
    There, now, son—of the man who mustered
    the army at Troy, son of Agamemnon:
    there it is—the land you have waited
    so many years to see with your own eyes.
    There is the ancient Argos you have pined for,
    the sacred land tormented Io fled;
    there, Orestes, you can see the market place
    that took its name from Apollo the wolf-killer;
    look leftward to the famous temple of Hera;
    stand here where we have at last arrived, and say   10
    this is Mycenae, this the city rich in gold,
    where the halls of Pelops' family ran with blood.
    A long time ago I carried you away
    from here, the scene of your father's murder;
    I took you out of your sister's care

and kept you alive and brought you up
to be the avenger of your father's death.
Now here we are. And so, Orestes, and you,
Pylades, best of friends, we can't waste time
deciding what our next move is. Listen: 20
the birds are loud because the sun is bright,
the black night and its dim starlight are gone.
So before anyone is up and out of the house
we'll make our plans; this is no time to wait:
let's keep on toward the thing we came to do.

ORESTES
Good friend, brave servant, anyone can see
how truly you have kept your faith with us.
You're like an old racehorse whose blood is up,
pricking his ears and prancing toward danger;
you push us on and stay right with us.   30
Now, here is what I have in mind. Listen closely,
and tell me if I've overlooked anything.
When I went to the Pythian oracle to find out
how to avenge the murder of my father,
Phoebus made this prophecy: alone, he said,
not with an army and all that goes with it,
but by stealth and by the strength of my own hand,
I would bring about this death, this justice.
Since that word is divine, we should proceed.
Go into the palace when you get the chance,   40
find out what they are doing, and bring back
a full report. They won't know you, your age
has changed you so they'll never suspect you.
Your story is that you are a foreigner,
from Phocis, with a message from their old friend
Phanoteus. Orestes is dead, you'll tell them,
and fill in the details as best you can—
a chariot wreck, say, in the Pythian games.

Right now, though, the god demands honor
to my father's tomb, with libations and a lock   50
of hair. Then we'll go back to the bramble thicket
where we hid that bronze urn, and we'll bring it
back here in our hands to help along our story,
false though it be, to please our audience:
that my body is no longer in this world,
but has gone up in flames and down to ashes.
What harm can it do me to fake my death
if that brings me another life and greater fame?
No word that causes good can be bad luck.
Wise men before now have falsified their deaths,   60
then risen to enjoy a hero's homecoming.
So I'm convinced this fable can make me live
and shine a light, like a star, on my enemies.
But oh, my homeland, gods of my native soil,
bless this my journey of revenge, and you also,
house of my fathers, stand with justice and the gods
by whose command I cleanse pollution from this place.
Let me not be sent away in disgrace, but let me
claim what is mine and rule over my own house.
Enough. Old friend, go do your work; we will   70
withdraw for now. This is one of those times
when all things point to the decisive act.

ELECTRA *(from inside the palace)*
    Oooooh, O god!

PAEDOGOGUS
    Listen, son—I think I heard somebody moaning
    inside that door—a servant girl, maybe.

ORESTES
    Is it poor Electra? Should we stay here and listen?

PAEDOGOGUS
    No, not at all. Before we do anything else, let us
    obey Apollo and pour libations to your father;
    that's the best first step toward a successful end.
    (Exeunt Paedogogus on the spectators' left, Orestes and Pylades on the
                        right. Enter Electra from the palace.)

ELECTRA
    O blessèd light,   80
    sweet air that joins the light
    over all the world,
    I cry again
    as you have heard me cry so many times before,
    and I strike my bleeding breast
    over and over, as each dark night
    gives way to morning.
    Even my pitiful bed remembers,
    there in that dreadful house,
    my long night-watches grieving   90
    my unlucky father who found
    no foreign resting place in war,
    but died when my mother
    and Aegisthus, her lover, took
    an axe to his head as a woodman does a tree.
    Murder! Yet I am the only one
    who mourns this act as we all should.
    I will not give up my cries,
    this bitter weeping,
    daylong, nightlong,   100
    while stars sweep brilliant shapes across the sky
    or fade away with morning.
    No! Like the nightingale
    that kills her children,
    I will make my endless cry
    to all who come before my father's door.
    O dark house of Hades and Persephone!

O Hermes of the dark spirits!
O you, mistress, the powerful Curse,
and you terrible daughters of the gods,   110
Erinyes, who know when a life
is taken and justice defied,
or when a marriage bed is fouled in secret!
Come! Help me! Find vengeance
for my father's murder, find my brother!
I have no more strength to bear up alone
under this deadly grief.
(Enter the Chorus of Argive women.)

CHORUS

Ah, child, Electra, child of a mother
most dismal among mothers, why
do you continue to waste away   120
in this useless grieving for Agamemnon,
so long ago caught and cut down
by unholy treachery
and your mother's murdering hand?
Let whoever did this be undone,
if it is not wrong to say it.

ELECTRA

Oh, good friends, good women,
you want to comfort me in my grief.
I know that as well as I know anything,
but I must keep up this mourning   130
for my father, and not give it up.
Dear women, friends in all our moods,
I beg you, please leave me to my grief.

CHORUS

This grieving will not bring your father back,
nor prayer, from the swamp of Hades where all must go.
No. When you go on too far with grief,

you come to endless anguish, and destroy yourself.
There is no salvation from your troubles here,
so why should you persist in suffering?

ELECTRA

Only a completely foolish child   140
could ever forget her father's horrible death.
No, I am more like that desolate nightingale,
messenger of Zeus, forever wailing—
"Itys! Itys!"—oh, she cries for her child, her Itys!
Or Niobe, suffering Niobe! To me you are divine,
weeping forever there in your stone grave.

CHORUS

Child, child, you are not all alone:
others endure overwhelming sorrow,
and some of them are in this house you share
with them, who share your ancestry,   150
your blood. Chrysothemis and Iphianassa
are still living, and so is another—
the child protected from all this pain,
who will come back to overjoyed Mycenae
in all the glory of his heritage,
escorted by the blessing of lord Zeus,
returning to his shining home: Orestes.

ELECTRA

Yes, my longing for him never stops.
I have no child, no husband, only
this flood of tears, this endless doom,   160
this grief. Meanwhile, he has forgotten
what he has heard or known of suffering.
How many times have I had word from him,
only to be let down? He wants to be here,
or so he says, and still he is not here.

CHORUS
> Bear up, child, be brave.
> Zeus in heaven is still all-powerful
> and sees and rules over everything that is.
> Give your unreasonable anger to him
> and do not rage too much   170
> against your enemies, or close
> the door of memory on them.
> Time brings relief, just as a god might.
> The son of Agamemnon remembers you
> as he waits in the pastures along the Crisa,
> and you are in the mind of the man himself
> as he stands, godlike, beside the Acheron.

ELECTRA
> But the best part of my life has left me
> and my strength and hope are failing;
> I shrivel beyond child-bearing   180
> with no man to protect me;
> I am like some unwanted guest, a slave almost,
> standing back from tables that are empty
> when my turn comes to sit down,
> a drab attendant in my father's house.

CHORUS
> Oh the cry, the sad outcry, the sad return,
> the sadness when he lay there unaware
> and the axe came straight down on him!
> Treachery planned, and passion carried through;
> together they bore and raised a hideous monster,   190
> whether the deed was done by god or human.

ELECTRA
> Oh that day, that hateful day,
> the worst of all the days that I have seen;
> Oh that night, that dreadful grief,

the unnameable feast itself,
where my father saw his death
carried to him in two hands,
two hands that stole my own life,
hands that left me for dead! I pray
for all the suffering Zeus can bring on them!   200
I pray they will never enjoy this opulence,
they, they, who did what they did!

CHORUS

Think now, and give your voice a rest.
Are you unable to see
how going on and on this way
takes you deep into a shameless grief
that you bring on yourself?
You give yourself no end of trouble,
waging this war within your soul,
your unforgiving soul. Bear up.   210
It is better not to argue or struggle
with those who have the power.

ELECTRA

My outrageous life has taught me how
to do outrageous things. I am not blind.
I know how it is with me, and yet
I am forced, compelled. I will keep it up,
this poisonous outcry,
as long as I have any breath.
Good women, sisters, would anyone
in his right mind try to comfort me?   220
Yes, you would. Leave me. Let me be.
There is no cure for this.
I will not rest from grief,
my countless tears, these cries.

CHORUS
    Still, I wish you well, like a mother
    you trust without question, and I tell you
    not to make fresh griefs out of old ones.

ELECTRA
    And where would you look to find a way
    to measure evil and suffering? Truly,
    when is it ever right to forsake the dead?   230
    Who would call that natural?
    If there are such people, I pray
    never to meet with their approval.
    If any good comes to me, I pray
    to find it hateful if I withhold
    the cries of grief, the tears, the honor
    my father deserves. If the dead man
    is doomed to lie there, going down
    to dust and miserable nothingness,
    and they live,   240
    that would mean the death of shame
    and the end of reverence for justice.

CHORUS
    I came here, child, thinking of you as well
    as myself. If I am wrong in what I say,
    then your way is the way that we will go.

ELECTRA
    Dear women! I am ashamed to have you think
    my laments are too many, my grief too much;
    but since I cannot help it, please forgive me.
    Could any well-born woman fail to grieve,
    watching the suffering in her father's house   250
    as I do, day and night, continually,
    while it grows worse and worse and is not eased?

First, my own mother who bore me has become
my worst enemy; then, here where I was raised,
I live side by side with my father's killers.
They are in charge of my life. They let me have
what I have, they deprive me of what I lack.
And finally, imagine how my days go by
when every one brings me the disgusting sight
of Aegisthus sitting on my father's throne,   260
or wearing the regal robes my father wore
and pouring libations on the very hearth
where he spilled my father's blood. Yet worst of all
is seeing that murderer in my father's bed
beside my outrageous mother, if mother she is
when she lies down to sleep beside that man.
She shares her daily life with that pollution,
as if no avenging spirit could punish her.
She even seems to flaunt what she has done,
marking the anniversary of the murder   270
with dances and sacrifices, slaughtering
cattle for the gods who have protected her.
But I am only a sad presence in the palace,
looking on and weeping, beaten down by grief,
grief and weeping at the blasphemous feast
named for my father, weeping to myself alone.
Even so, my grief can never have free rein,
because her voice is always at my ear,
the voice of this creature, this so-called queen,
spitting one hard insult after another.   280
"Evil, hateful girl," she says, "is no one else
an orphan daughter? Are you the only one?
I wish you a hard death, and an eternity
of mourning, deep among the gods below!"
That is how she treats me, unless she hears
some rumor that Orestes is coming. Then
she stands before me in a rage, and shouts,

"Aren't you the one I have to thank for this?
The one who took Orestes from my hands
and smuggled him away? This is your work!   290
The time will come when you must pay for this!"
She barks that sort of thing, and all the while
her noble bridegroom stands by in brave support—
this weakling, this disease, this coward
who recruits women to fight with him.
So on I wait for Orestes to come home
and end this torture. Meanwhile, my heart breaks
because he is forever about to be here,
and my hopes are being ground away to nothing.
Oh, friends, dear women, when things are as they are,   300
there is no place for reverence or good sense;
in evil times we walk an evil road.

CHORUS

    Tell me, is Aegisthus nearby as you speak,
    or is he away from home?

ELECTRA

                         He is away, of course.
    You don't believe I'd come out if he were here;
    he is in the country.

CHORUS

                Then might I speak freely?

ELECTRA

    He is away, so you may ask me what you like.

CHORUS

    I would be glad to know what news you have
    of your brother, whether he is coming soon
    or still putting it off; that is my question.   310

ELECTRA

He says he'll come, but in spite of promises
he still doesn't do what he says he will do.

CHORUS

A man will sometimes hesitate before
the prospect of a major undertaking.

ELECTRA

Well, I didn't hesitate to save him.

CHORUS

Have faith. He has a brave and loyal nature.

ELECTRA

Without faith, I would not have lived this long.

CHORUS

No more for now. I see Chrysothemis,
your sister, child of the same father—and mother—
coming out of the palace with offerings   320
in her hands, gifts for the spirits of the dead.
(Enter Chrysothemis.)

CHRYSOTHEMIS

Sister! What are you doing out of the palace?
What are you going to say, here in the open?
Is no time long enough for you to learn
to keep your useless anger to yourself?
I know my own anger, too, and my grief
at how things are; if I were strong enough,
I would speak out, but in a dangerous time
I need to turn a little with the wind
and not take mundane rashness for true nerve.   330
I wish you had it in you to do the same.

I know there's more pure justice in your way
of seeing these things than there is in mine,
but my freedom depends on my ability
to recognize a power greater than ours.

ELECTRA

Disgusting! You, the daughter of your father,
set him aside in favor of your mother,
who gives you the opinions you express;
they aren't truly your own. Take your choice—
be mistaken or be correct—but be aware: 340
your wisdom would betray the ones you love.
You just now said that if you had the strength
you'd let them know just how much you hate them,
but when I devote myself to my father's memory
you're not only not with me; you're against me.
Must you add cowardice to all your troubles?
So tell me, or let me tell you, what good
could come to me if I set down my grief.
I live—not well, but well enough for me.
Meanwhile, whatever trouble I can cause them   350
may possibly give honor to the dead,
if there is pleasure where the dead have gone.
You say you hate them, but words are all you have
for hatred of them; in everything you do,
you lend support to your father's murderers.
That is not my way. I would not side with them
even to have the luxuries you enjoy.
You can have your delicacies and your comfort;
my comfort is in not making myself sick.
I don't want what you have. Neither would you,   360
if you saw more clearly; as it is, you choose
not to be called after that noblest father;
you'd rather be known as your mother's child.
People will see your treachery for what it is,
the betrayal of your father and your family.

CHORUS
　　Never let anger tell you what to say.
　　There is wisdom in you both; you ought to find
　　a way to take turns learning from each other.

CHRYSOTHEMIS
　　Dear friends, I am quite accustomed to her way
　　of talking, and would not have brought this up　　　　370
　　if I hadn't heard of a fresh evil, and plans
　　to keep her and her lamentations quiet.

ELECTRA
　　Then tell me. If what you heard is any worse
　　than what I suffer now, I'll stop arguing.

CHRYSOTHEMIS
　　I'll tell you what I know. If you keep up
　　this public mourning, they propose to send you
　　far away, even beyond sight of the sun:
　　an exile, shut up in a windowless room
　　where you may have your griefs, and time to grieve.
　　Think now; don't blame me later if you suffer.　　　　380
　　Act like a sensible person while you can.

ELECTRA
　　This—this is what they really plan to do?

CHRYSOTHEMIS
　　It really is—when Aegisthus returns.

ELECTRA
　　Well, all right, then. I hope he gets back soon.

CHRYSOTHEMIS
　　Poor sister, do you know what you are asking?

ELECTRA
Yes: let him hurry, if you're right about his plans.

CHRYSOTHEMIS
So you can suffer—what? Have you gone crazy?

ELECTRA
So I can suffer—not your wretched presence.

CHRYSOTHEMIS
No love at all for such life as you have?

ELECTRA
Why, certainly! My life is one long pleasure!   390

CHRYSOTHEMIS
And yet it could be, if you kept your head.

ELECTRA
Don't advise me to desert those dearest to me.

CHRYSOTHEMIS
No, I advise you to know when you're beaten.

ELECTRA
You're welcome to be meek. It's not my way.

CHRYSOTHEMIS
There's honor in not letting madness defeat you.

ELECTRA
If I'm defeated, I'll still honor my father.

CHRYSOTHEMIS
Still, I believe our father understands . . .

ELECTRA
>Cowards would understand what you are saying.

CHRYSOTHEMIS
>But you're no coward, and you understand.

ELECTRA
>Not I. I hope I never believe that.   400

CHRYSOTHEMIS
>Then I'll go on with what I came to do.

ELECTRA
>And what is that? Who will receive these gifts?

CHRYSOTHEMIS
>Mother sends these libations to our father.

ELECTRA
>What? Libations for her worst enemy on earth?

CHRYSOTHEMIS
>The man her own hand killed, you'd rather say.

ELECTRA
>Some friend suggested this? Who thought of it?

CHRYSOTHEMIS
>I think a nightmare brought this fear on her.

ELECTRA
>My father's gods, at least be with me now!

CHRYSOTHEMIS
>Do you take some kind of courage from her fear?

ELECTRA
>If you can describe her dream, then I can say.   410

CHRYSOTHEMIS
    I only know a little—no details.

ELECTRA
    Then tell me what you know. A little news
    sometimes makes all the difference in a crisis.

CHRYSOTHEMIS
    They say that my—that is, our father returned
    to be with her a while in the world of light,
    and took in hand the staff he used to carry,
    the one Aegisthus uses now, and planted it
    beside the hearth, where it became a tree
    with shade enough to cover all Mycenae.
    I heard that much from someone who was there   420
    as she told the dream over to the sunrise.
    That's all, except the fear that tortures her
    and makes her send me out with offerings.
    I feel that fear, and wish that you did, too,
    rather than this mindless certainty.
    You're reckless now, but you'll need me again.

ELECTRA
    Dear sister, do not let these things you carry
    pass out of your hands to the tomb. It is not right.
    No law, human or divine, says you must act
    on behalf of our father's wretched wife   430
    and carry her libations to his tomb.
    Let the wind have them, bury them in the dust,
    but don't let them touch our father's resting place.
    Keep them safely buried for when her time comes!
    She must have the smallest conscience among women,
    or she would not have thought of making offerings
    at a tomb where her own murder victim lies.
    Consider: would the dead man in that grave
    receive such offerings gladly from this woman
    who had the nerve to kill him monstrously,   440

dismembering him as if he were an enemy
and wiping off the bloodstains with his hair?
These offerings: are they enough to pardon her?
Impossible. Get rid of them, and cut
a lock of hair from your head and from mine,
unhappy as I am that this poor gift
is all I have: dull hair, and this plain sash.
Kneel there, and pray to him that he may rise
in all his kindness from the underworld
and bring us help against our enemies.   450
Pray also for the triumph of Orestes,
that he may live to trample on his foe
and bring the day when we honor our father
with richer gifts in our hands than we have now.
It was his thought that sent her this nightmare;
remember that, my dear, and for our sake
do as I say. Do this for him we love,
our father watching from the underworld.

CHORUS

This girl has spoken from a righteous heart;
yours, my dear, should lead you accordingly.   460

CHRYSOTHEMIS

And so it does. Whenever a choice is right,
it makes sense that there be no argument,
but quick action. Yet, when I do this, friends,
I beg you not to speak of it. My mother,
if she finds out, could make me regret my courage.
(*Exit Chrysothemis.*)

CHORUS

If madness has not warped my clairvoyance,
if I was not born a false prophet,
Justice has sent a sign
and Justice is coming, holding victory in her hands.

Before long, my child, she will bear down on them.   470
My mind is set in faith
now that I have heard this dream
whose sweet breath comes to touch us.
You father, that great lord of Greeks,
will not ever forget,
nor will that two-edged axe forget!
That bronze still holds the shame
of your father's brutal death.
On countless feet she comes, her countless hands
preparing her a vengeful ambush,   480
the Fury shod in bronze.
She rises up against an unholy marriage,
a doomed bridal night in the bed of the damned,
a forbidden coupling!
Yes, my mind is set in faith
that this sign did not come down
to bring these evil people joy.
No prophecy comes true
in any dreaming human life
if this dream should fail   490
to bring its truth out of the dark.
Ah, the grief goes back so far!
Oh, treacherous horsemanship,
that cheating ride of Pelops
long ago!
Ah, ghastly inheritance!
Since the fall of Myrtilus
from his chariot of gold
down to the waves,
down to eternal sleep,   500
the torture
of unceasing grief holds on
forever to this house of doom.
(Enter Clytemnestra with an attendant who carries a basket of fruits as
offerings.)

CLYTEMNESTRA
On the loose again, are you? So it seems.
That is because Aegisthus is not here.
He could always keep you from going out
to embarrass your family in public. He's away,
and you can ignore me. Over and over,
you tell anyone at all that I am a tyrant,
corrupt, violent, torturing you and yours.   510
I do no harm; I only speak hard words,
and those are mere return for what you seem
so fond of saying to me, and your excuse
never varies: it is your father, your father,
how he died by my hand. Yes, mine. I know it.
I can't deny it. But it was justice, too,
not only I, that caught up with him at last.
You'd understand this if you had good sense.
That precious father you are always grieving—
he was the only man of all the Greeks   520
who could bring himself to sacrifice your sister,
give her to the gods, though his begetting her
cost him far less than did my bearing her.
Now then: for whose good was that sacrifice?
Will you say it was for the Argives' sake?
They had no right to her; she was my daughter.
Or say it was to please his brother Menelaus;
is there no penalty due me for that?
Didn't Menelaus have two children of his own?
Either of them would have been fit sacrifice,   530
since their parents brought about the expedition.
Did Hades want my child instead of hers?
Or did your despicable father find he had
greater love for those children than for mine?
Does this not show you mindless cruelty?
I think so; and the girl who died would, too,
if she could speak. That is why what I did
rests lightly on my conscience. I suggest
that you stop blaming me, and learn good sense.

ELECTRA

    This time you can't say I was first to speak   540
    some cruelty that makes you speak it back.
    I hope you will allow me now to tell the truth
    about the dead man and my sister, too.

CLYTEMNESTRA

    By all means. If when you spoke you always
    led off that way, you'd be less painful to hear.

ELECTRA

    Then I will tell it. You say you killed my father.
    Could you make any more disgraceful confession,
    whether or not there was justice in the act?
    I say there was none in your killing him;
    there was only the urging of the evil man   550
    who shares your bed. Ask Artemis the huntress
    what act she punished when she brought fair winds
    to move the ships that lay becalmed at Aulis—
    or let me tell you, since she does not speak.
    My father, so they say, was amusing himself
    hunting in a grove sacred to Artemis,
    and started a dappled stag with a handsome rack.
    As he killed it, he happened to drop a phrase
    of sacrilegious pride, and in her anger
    the goddess delayed the Greeks until the death   560
    of the beast was paid for when my father made
    the sacrifice of his daughter. That was why
    he sacrificed her; there was no other way
    to free the army—either to go home
    or to go to Troy. He sacrificed the girl
    because of that, and much against his will,
    after trying all he could to get out of it.
    Not for Menelaus. But let us see it
    your way for a moment; let us say
    he made the sacrifice for his brother's sake.   570
    Did that make it right for you to kill him?

By what law? Be careful that you don't invoke
some law that calls you to fatal account:
a law that says we take a life for a life
would put you next in line for final justice.
But beware of an excuse that has no force.
Tell me, if you will, what wrong you put right
by going without shame into the bed of a man
whose hands are stained with my father's blood,
bearing his children and turning your back   580
on faithful children born to a righteous union?
What good is there to say about these things?
Or would you claim them as entitlements
because you lost your daughter? That's outrageous,
if it is what you think. It is not honorable
to sleep with your enemy for your daughter's sake.
But no, there is no criticizing you,
who find so many ways of accusing me
of hurting you. You're not so much my mother
as my mistress, keeping me under your thumb,   590
and his too, your . . . mate. Meanwhile another life
goes on just as miserably, and far away:
Orestes, who barely escaped from your hard hand.
You are fond of saying I brought him up
to punish you; that's what I would have done,
I assure you, if I had been strong enough.
As far as that is concerned, advertise
whatever you like about me: shamelessness,
evil, gall, let the world hear about it.
If that is my way, I came by it honestly.   600

CHORUS *(to Clytemnestra)*
I can see the anger in your breath, but not
your thoughts on whether she is making sense.

CLYTEMNESTRA
And what kind of thoughts am I supposed to have
for a grown woman who mistreats her mother?
Are you thinking that she might behave herself?

ELECTRA
> You ought to know that I am ashamed of this,
> even if you don't think so. I know what is wrong
> for someone like me, someone my age. But the anger
> that comes from you, the things you do to me,
> make me act the way I do, against my will.   610
> I have learned evil from an evil teacher.

CLYTEMNESTRA
> You *are* scandalous. To be sure, my words
> and what I do have made you talk too much.

ELECTRA
> I speak your speech because you act as you do.
> Words can be found even for acts of yours.

CLYTEMNESTRA
> I swear by Artemis that you'll give up
> this arrogance when Aegisthus comes back.

ELECTRA
> You see? You can't control your anger even when
> you say I may speak freely. You can't listen.

CLYTEMNESTRA
> Will you spoil even my sacrifice with contempt,   620
> with this precious license to say anything?

ELECTRA
> Please. Pray proceed with your sacrifice.
> Do not denounce my voice; I will not speak.

CLYTEMNESTRA *(addressing first the servant who holds the offerings)*
> Now, you lift up this orchard offering,
> so I can pray to this image of our lord
> to be set free from the fears I suffer.
(addressing the statue)

O Apollo our protector, hear me now,
though I speak secretly and low, because
I am not among friends, but in a place
where it would not be good to reveal too much   630
while she stands there with her overworked voice,
on fire to spread rumors through the city.
So hear me even though I speak this way.
Bring to pass, O god of light, the two visions
that came to me in dreams last night—provided
they mean good things; if they foretell some harm,
turn them on those who do not wish me well.
If somewhere someone plans to steal my riches,
stop them, and let me stay here from now on
in safety, queen of the house of Atreus   640
and its lands, living at peace among my friends
and those of my children who wish me no pain.
Oh hear my prayer, Apollo of the Light,
and hear as well the prayers I do not speak;
you know them, for a child of Zeus knows all.
(Enter the Paedogogus.)

PAEDOGOGUS
   Good ladies, can you tell me—have I found
   the house of king Aegisthus?

CHORUS
   This is it, sir; you have found the place yourself.

PAEDOGOGUS
   And am I right to assume this is his lady?
   She seems a queen.

CHORUS
                        Correct, sir; this is she.   650

PAEDOGOGUS

    Your Highness, greetings! I come from a friend
    with good news for Aegisthus and for you.

CLYTEMNESTRA

    You and your greeting are welcome; but tell me,
    who is this friend whose messenger you are?

PAEDOGOGUS

    Phanoteus the Phocian, passing on urgent news.

CLYTEMNESTRA

    And what is it, then? Speak. Coming from a friend,
    you carry, I am sure, a friendly message.

PAEDOGOGUS

    Orestes is dead. In brief, that is it.

ELECTRA

    Oh, god, not that! Now everything is over!

CLYTEMNESTRA

    How's that, how's that, stranger? Ignore her.   660

PAEDOGOGUS

    I said then, and say now: Orestes is dead.

ELECTRA

    Oh, god, no more! I am destroyed!

CLYTEMNESTRA *(to Electra)*

                            You,

    mind your own business!
(to the Paedogogus)

                        But you, stranger,
    tell me exactly how he came to die.

PAEDOGOGUS
    I'll tell you everything; that is why I came.
    Orestes made his way to the Delphic shrine
    to enter those games that are the pride of Greece.
    The herald first called runners to the footrace,
    and he came on the course, his splendid body
    admired by everyone. He took the lead   670
    right at the start and held it all the way.
    To say it all as quickly as I can,
    I do not know a man who has matched him
    in triumphant acts of strength and skill,
    but this is clear: in all announced results,
    his name came first, and people envied him
    each time they heard the herald call him Argive,
    Orestes by name, and Agamemnon's son—
    son of the man who led that host of Greeks.
    So, for awhile, things went that way for him.   680
    But human strength is nothing to the gods;
    a day came when at sunrise race-horses
    were hitched to chariots and took the course;
    he was there along with all the others.
    One was an Achaean, and one was Spartan;
    there were two drivers from Libya, and fifth
    came Orestes, driving mares from Thessaly.
    Sixth was an Aetolian with chestnut colts;
    a Magnesian was the seventh, and the eighth
    was an Aenian with white horses. Ninth,   690
    a man from Athens, city of the gods;
    the tenth and final driver was Boeotian.
    They put their chariots under starter's orders
    and took positions given them by lot.
    When the bronze trumpet sounded, they were off.
    They shouted at their horses, shook the reins,
    and a rumbling dust-cloud lifted from the course
    and pulsed with the rattling of the chariots—
    a crowded, tight-packed charge of men with whips
    trying to break from the tangled hubs and horses.   700

Behind them and beside their wheels the breath
and lathered foam of horses wheezed and spattered.
Orestes drove to hug the turning-post, almost
grazing it every time with his inside wheel,
checking his inside horse, letting the other run.
So far all chariots were still up and rolling.
But then the Aenian's hard-mouthed colts,
coming out of the turn into the seventh lap,
got out of his control and crashed head first
into the Libyan—the one from Barca. This   710
started a pileup, chariots crashing one
after the other, until the whole race-course
of Crisa churned with chariot-wreckage.
The Athenian driver was alert enough
to see all this and make a clever move:
he pulled aside and let the flood go by.
Orestes, too, had stayed just off the pace,
trusting the last lap to bring him home in front.
But when he saw the race was down to him
and the Athenian, he gave a shout that rang   720
his horses' ears, and took out after him.
Yoke to yoke they raced, one pulling ahead
for a few strides, then the other. Up to now
Orestes had driven safely through each lap
and kept his chariot's wheels on the ground.
Then he slipped and let the left rein go slack
halfway through a turn, and hit the pillar,
cracked the axle box in two, and spilled out
over the chariot-rail, tangled in the long reins,
and his horses dragged him all over the course.   730
The whole crowd screamed, watching this young man
who had won so much and then had such bad luck,
bouncing over the hard ground until charioteers
reined in his charging horses and cut him loose,
so mangled that his friends would not have known him.
They made a pyre and burned him right away,

and Phocian men appointed to the task
now bring this lowly dust, once a mighty man,
in a small bronze urn for burial at home.
That was it—horrible just to hear, but for us   740
who saw it, the greatest sorrow I have seen.

CHORUS

Oh, terrible. The whole line of our ancient lords
has been wiped out, it seems, down to the roots.

CLYTEMNESTRA

Oh, god, what now? Is this good news, or terrible,
but for my good? It makes for bitter pain,
this staying alive by my own suffering.

PAEDOGOGUS

But lady, why does my message make you sad?

CLYTEMNESTRA

There is a mystery in motherhood. Even when
they make her suffer, one cannot hate her children.

PAEDOGOGUS

It seems that I have made a useless journey.   750

CLYTEMNESTRA

No, not useless; why should you call it useless?
You have brought me absolute proof of his death.
His life grew out of mine, but he turned away,
rejected my breast and care, a fugitive
cut off from me. Once he was gone, he saw
no more of me, but blamed me for the death
of his father, and made poisonous threats
that found their way to me, so gentle sleep
could never shelter me at night or in the daytime,

since each moment felt as if it could be my last.   760
But now that I have been set free from fear—
fear of him, and her, too, a worse threat still,
living with me but draining my blood, too—
now, despite her threats, I see a peaceful life.

ELECTRA

Oh, god, no worse! Now, Orestes, this disaster
is mine to mourn; this woman here, your own mother,
insults you even in death. Splendid, is it not?

CLYTEMNESTRA

Certainly not for you; for him, just so.

ELECTRA

Oh, let divine revenge hear what she says!

CLYTEMNESTRA

She who should hear has heard, and chosen well.   770

ELECTRA

Insult me now, since luck is on your side.

CLYTEMNESTRA

You and Orestes won't stop me now, will you?

ELECTRA

We are the ones who are stopped; we can't stop you.

CLYTEMNESTRA

Stranger, you could have earned a rich reward
if you had stopped her endless stream of talk.

PAEDOGOGUS

If all is well, I should be on my way.

CLYTEMNESTRA
>Not at all; that would be less than you deserve,
>to say nothing of the friend who sent you here.
>Come in. Leave her and her complaints outside.
>*(Clytemnestra, her attendant, and the Paedogogus go into the palace.)*

ELECTRA
>Do you suppose that wretched woman feels   780
>true pain in those dreadful wails for her dead son?
>No. She has gone in triumph, and my heart breaks.
>Dearest Orestes, your death murders me!
>You have snatched out of my heart the last hopes
>I still cherished, that someday you would come
>to avenge our father and my poor lost self.
>But where can I go now? I am alone,
>and have you no longer, nor my father.
>Now as before I must live as a slave
>among my enemies, my father's killers.   790
>So things are truly splendid, are they not?
>But from now on I will not spend my days
>living with those people in that house. No.
>I will lie down alone before these gates
>and waste away. Let him who hates that sight
>come from the palace and kill me. It will be
>a joy to die and none to live. I can't keep on.

CHORUS
>Where is the lightning of Zeus, where
>is the blazing sun, if they can look
>at this and hide it from themselves?   800

ELECTRA
>Ah, ah, ai ai!

CHORUS
>Child, why are you weeping?

ELECTRA
    Aaaiii!

CHORUS
    Don't cry out so!

ELECTRA
    You will finish me!

CHORUS
    How?

ELECTRA
    Saying that any hope may come
    from the dead is like putting your foot
    on my neck as I fade away.

CHORUS
    I remember that the great Amphiaraus   810
    was destroyed by women's necklaces,
    yet now, below the earth—

ELECTRA
    Ah, ah god!

CHORUS
    —he is a king, whole among lost souls.

ELECTRA
    Alas!

CHORUS
    Alas is right, for that murderess—

ELECTRA
                                —Killed!

CHORUS

                                                    Yes!

ELECTRA

I know, I know! But a hero
came to the aid of that grieving woman; for me
there is no hero; the one I had is taken away.

CHORUS

Your fate has brought you grief.

ELECTRA

I have learned this too, learned it too well,   820
from the flood of hateful things that is my life,
this flood no season interrupts.

CHORUS

We are your witnesses.

ELECTRA

Then please don't encourage me in—

CHORUS

In what?

ELECTRA

—the faith that comes from dreaming
of rescue, kinship with a noble hero.

CHORUS

Death comes to all who live.

ELECTRA

Must all the living die among
the smashing hooves of racehorses,   830
dragged, strangling, in the reins?

CHORUS
Too horrible to bear!

ELECTRA
So it is; if in a foreign country,
beyond reach of my hands—

CHORUS
Oh, no . . .

ELECTRA
he has gone down beyond my touch,
my final care of him.
(Enter Chrysothemis.)

CHRYSOTHEMIS
Oh, dear sister, happy news has made me forget
my dignity! I have even been running—
to bring it here to you, because it means
an end to all the suffering you've endured.   840

ELECTRA
Where would you find any help for me,
when it is impossible to imagine any?

CHRYSOTHEMIS
Orestes is here. No, listen to me!
It must be! Just as I am standing here!

ELECTRA
Oh, poor child, have you lost your mind?
Have you decided to make light of our grief?

CHRYSOTHEMIS
No, I swear! By our father's hearth, I make
no jokes. I tell you, he is here with us!

ELECTRA

Oh, god. So who on earth could have told you
this story, and so easily made you believe it?   850

CHRYSOTHEMIS

No one else has told me anything; I believe
what I say because of things I have seen myself.

ELECTRA

What proves it? What have you seen? What spark
has set your thoughts on fire this way?

CHRYSOTHEMIS

Just listen, please, so you can hear it from me
and then decide whether I make sense or not.

ELECTRA

Well, tell the story, then, if it makes you happy.

CHRYSOTHEMIS

All right. I will tell you everything I saw.
I came to the ancient tomb where our father lies,
and saw at the top of the mound fresh streams of milk   860
that had recently been poured, and on his grave
a garland made of all the flowers now in bloom.
I stopped and wondered, then, and looked around
for anyone else who might be watching me.
But there was nothing there but peaceful stillness,
so I approached the tomb, and on the edge
of the vault I saw it—a fresh-cut lock of hair.
At that moment—heaven!—brightness came over me
that I was seeing a trace of him—Orestes!
I took it in my hands and did not speak,   870
but let the tears come to my eyes. I know
right now, as I did then, that he alone

had left this tribute on the grave. Who else,
aside from me and you, cares for that tomb?
Neither of us had left those offerings.
I know I didn't, and how could you, since you
can't safely leave the palace even for worship's sake?
And our mother? Well, that is not her way,
and even if it were, we would have known it.
No. Orestes alone has left these offerings.   880
So have courage, my dear sister. The same fate
does not stay forever with the same people;
our fate has been despicable before now,
but today, perhaps, will bring us blessings.

ELECTRA
    Oh, god, how sad, how foolish—I pity you!

CHRYSOTHEMIS
    What is it? You don't think this is good news?

ELECTRA
    You wander—on foot and in your mind—and don't know
           where.

CHRYSOTHEMIS
    How can I be wrong about what I have seen myself?

ELECTRA
    Oh, poor girl, he is dead, and there is no chance
    that he will save us. Don't look to him for help.   890

CHRYSOTHEMIS
    My god. And who in the world has told you this?

ELECTRA
    I heard it from the man who saw him die.

CHRYSOTHEMIS
    And where is he? My mind can't take it in.

ELECTRA
    Inside. He is our mother's welcome guest.
    He has brought her no grief.

CHRYSOTHEMIS
                              No, no. Who was it,
    then, who put those offerings on my father's tomb?

ELECTRA
    I think someone must have put them there
    in memory of Orestes and his death.

CHRYSOTHEMIS
    God, no end! And I was running here
    so happy with my news, with no idea,   900
    after all, what our predicament is.
    I find our old griefs, and new ones added to them.

ELECTRA
    That is how things are. But let yourself
    do as I say, and we can look for some relief.

CHRYSOTHEMIS
    Shall I bring back the dead into the light?

ELECTRA
    I didn't say that. I am not a fool.

CHRYSOTHEMIS
    Of the things in my power, which should I do?

ELECTRA
    As I suggested, let me be your guide.

CHRYSOTHEMIS
   I can do anything that will do some good.

ELECTRA
   The thing we want to do will not be easy.   910

CHRYSOTHEMIS
   I know. Count on all the strength I have.

ELECTRA
   Good. Here's what I have decided to do.
   You know, as I do, that we have no allies
   in this situation; Hades has taken all there were,
   and we are alone. As long as I kept getting word
   that my brother was alive and healthy, it made sense
   to hope he'd come someday to take revenge
   for his father's murder. Now he is gone for good,
   and I turn to you: do not be afraid
   to join with me, your sister, to accomplish   920
   the death of our father's murderer, Aegisthus.
   That's it. I have no secrets from you now.
   But how long will you stand by, doing nothing?
   What hope can you look to that isn't dead?
   By now, you've earned the right to condemn the loss
   of your father's estate, to grieve the passing years
   that brought you to this age without a bridal song,
   beyond hope of marriage, beyond all hope
   of ever enjoying such things. Aegisthus is no fool:
   he'll do all he can to keep offspring of ours   930
   from growing up to bring him vengeful grief.
   Look: if you go along with me in this plan,
   praise for your piety will come from the dead,
   from both our father and our brother; then
   your fame as a free woman, born to nobility,
   will attract a worthy mate. Nobility
   is admired by everyone. Imagine, besides,

the glory you will earn, along with me,
if we do this. Who wouldn't praise us for it?
People will point us out and tell our story,   940
how we took possession of our paternal rights
at the risk of our own lives, going against
powerful enemies, and took bloody revenge.
"Let everyone honor them," people will say,
"and applaud their bravery, so like a warrior's,
and give them praise at public ceremonies."
All the world will say these things about us,
and our fame will live forever after us.
Come. Sister. Be with me. Be with your father,
shoulder beside your brother's shoulder, bring   950
deliverance from my griefs as well as yours,
and avoid the shame of mere skulking survival.

CHORUS

At such difficult times, foresight and prudence
strengthen advice both given and received.

CHRYSOTHEMIS

True, ladies; and if she had good sense, she might
have been cautious instead of speaking recklessly;
but she lacks good sense. What good can you see
in arming yourself so rashly, and recruiting me?
Can't you see? You are a woman, not a man,
and hand to hand, your enemies are stronger,   960
and grow stronger every day, while our fortunes
dwindle away to nothing. Who in the world
could kill such a man and get away with it?
Be careful! Bad as they are, things would be worse
if what we're saying now were overheard.
What good is any fame—shining or not—
if miserable execution takes us there?
Still, there are worse things than death to be endured:
one is wanting death, and lacking the power to die.

No. I beg you. Before we are completely wiped out,   970
ourselves and our family extinct, rein yourself in.
All you have said to me will be my secret,
and won't come back to harm you. At long last,
you must get hold of yourself, have good sense,
and accept the greater power, since yours is gone.

CHORUS

Take that to heart. There is nothing in the world
more valuable than prudence and discretion.

ELECTRA

Nothing you have said surprises me. I knew
perfectly well that you'd dismiss my proposal.
So my hand alone will have to do this thing: 980
I won't stand by and let it go undone.

CHRYSOTHEMIS

My god.
I wish your aims had been so bravely set
when our father died. You could do anything.

ELECTRA

My nature was the same, but I understood less.

CHRYSOTHEMIS

Let such understanding lead you to long life.

ELECTRA

Your sermon preaches unwillingness to act.

CHRYSOTHEMIS

That is correct. The attempt will surely fail.

ELECTRA

I envy your discretion and despise your cowardice.

CHRYSOTHEMIS

When you say that to praise me, I will endure it.   990

ELECTRA

You will never need to endure such praise from me.

CHRYSOTHEMIS

We still have plenty of time to see about that.

ELECTRA

Leave me alone. You're no help at all to me.

CHRYSOTHEMIS

I am, but you don't have the sense to see it.

ELECTRA

Go ahead and let your mother in on this.

CHRYSOTHEMIS

No. I'm not angry enough with you to do that.

ELECTRA

But enough to watch someone humiliate me.

CHRYSOTHEMIS

Not that so much as hope for your safety.

ELECTRA

Am I obliged to see this exactly as you do?

CHRYSOTHEMIS

Yes, for now. When you come to your senses, lead on.   1000

ELECTRA

It's sad to hear cleverness being wrong.

CHRYSOTHEMIS

This trouble you see so clearly is your own.

ELECTRA

    Are you so sure that I am in the wrong?

CHRYSOTHEMIS

    Sometimes being right is harm enough.

ELECTRA

    That's not a rule I would care to live by.

CHRYSOTHEMIS

    If you keep on, you will come to see things my way.

ELECTRA

    Well, I will keep on; you don't frighten me.

CHRYSOTHEMIS

    Is that the way things stand? You'll go ahead?

ELECTRA

    I will. There's nothing worse than being wrong.

CHRYSOTHEMIS

    You don't understand me. You don't hear me.   1010

ELECTRA

    I made up my mind about this long ago.

CHRYSOTHEMIS

    I give up, then. I'll go, since you despise
    the things I say, and I despise your choice.

ELECTRA

    Go on, then. My way is not your way, whatever
    your wishes might be. It's pure foolishness
    even to wish for what can never be.

CHRYSOTHEMIS
    Well, if this is what you consider good sense,
    keep on considering, until your mistakes
    lead you back here, to everything I've said.
(Exit Chrysothemis.)

CHORUS
    Why is this? Look, the birds of the air   1020
    are wise enough to nurture those
    who gave them life, and come from them,
    while we neglect to pay those dues.
    Why? Now our failure is found out,
    punished by the thunderbolt of Zeus
    and the sacred anger of Themis. Listen!
    Rumor, voice that goes among men alive on earth,
    carry the word beneath the earth
    to that descendant of Atreus—
    let Agamemnon know: there is dishonor here,   1030
    shame beyond ceremonial absolution.
    Let word go below that their house now
    is plagued! A double strife tears
    the children from a loving way of life.
    Now one daughter is bereaved, alone
    on the open sea, forever grieving
    her father's fate, forever weeping
    like the nightingale, indifferent
    to death, ready for the dark
    if only she can bring an end   1040
    to the twin furies who have hemmed her in.
    What father could have sired such loyalty?
    Oh, child, child, nobility
    never gives in to humiliating survival.
    Still, you have taken on
    a destiny full of grief,
    avoiding false defense of depravity
    for the mere sake of reputation

for both nobility and wisdom.
May your turn come to be triumphant   1050
over your enemies, to rise above them
as far as you are now below them.   ·
For I have come upon you
as you take a perilous road,
yet, under the highest laws,
winning the highest prize—because
you keep your holy devotion to great Zeus.
(*Enter Orestes with Pylades and two attendants.*)

ORESTES
  Your pardon, ladies, have we had good directions?
  Are we on the road to what we are looking for?

CHORUS
  What are you looking for? What brings you here?   1060

ORESTES
  I have been asking after the home of Aegisthus.

CHORUS
  And this is it. Whoever directed you owes you nothing.

ORESTES
  In that case, which of you would be so good
  as to announce our long-awaited arrival?

CHORUS (*indicating Electra*)
  She, if you need to speak to the next of kin.

ORESTES
  Good lady, go in, then, and give the word
  that Aegisthus has visitors from Phocis.

ELECTRA
  Oh, god. Surely you do not bring proof
  of the terrible rumor we have heard?

ORESTES

> I am unaware of your rumor, but old Strophius   1070
> entrusted me with the news about Orestes.

ELECTRA

> What is it, sir? Oh, I am so afraid!

ORESTES

> He is dead, and what little is left of him
> we carried here contained in this small urn.

ELECTRA

> Aaah! This is what we heard; now it is here.
> My burden and my grief have come to hand.

ORESTES

> If you would weep over Orestes' trials,
> know that his body rests within this urn.

ELECTRA

> Oh, stranger, sir, I beg you, let me hold it
> in my hands if truly it holds him; then   1080
> I can mourn for myself and the whole family.

ORESTES *(to Pylades)*

> Pass it over to her, whoever she may be.
> She asks without demanding, peaceably,
> as if she were a friend or relative.

ELECTRA

> Oh, this is all there is of you, a remnant
> of the life that meant the most to me—
> Orestes, you took my high hopes with you
> and now you bring them back, forever destroyed.
> Now there is nothing left of you but this
> that I can hold in my two hands; oh, child,   1090

you were so alive the day I sent you off from home;
now, I wish I had died instead of stealing you
and handing you over to protection from murder,
and seeing you safely off to a foreign country;
it would have been better if you had died
and taken a place that day in our father's tomb.
Now you have died alone, an exile, far
from your home, far from your sister, and I—
the ceaseless mourner—stare at my idle hands
that neither washed your body nor picked out   1100
your sad remains from the embers of the pyre.
Instead, poor thing, your body has been tended
by strangers' hands, reduced to a light burden
in this little urn. My baby. All my care
is nothing now, all I did and loved to do.
You were no more your mother's than you were mine,
and the housemaids were not your nurses; I was.
When you called "Sister" you always meant me.
Now in one day all this has disappeared,
as if you were a whirlwind taking dust away.   1110
Our father is dead; my life is over, and you
are dead and gone. Our enemies are laughing
and our mother is insanely, evilly rejoicing,
though you often sent secret messages to say
that you would come and have revenge on her.
But our unkind fate, mine and yours, has brought
destruction to all that, and brought at last
these ashes and a memory, not your living self.
Ah, ah, my—
my poor, you poor body,   1120
oh, the fearful road you came,
oh, god, my dearest one, the end of me,
yes, the end of me, my brother. Now take me with you.
Let me be with you in this last home of yours,
let nothingness have me since I am nothing,
let me be with you in death from now on.

When you were alive, we shared our fate,
and now I want to die and share your tomb.
I know now: death is the end of suffering.

CHORUS
Your are the child of a human father, Electra;   1130
Orestes was human; remember that and grieve
a little less. We all pay this last debt.

ORESTES
Oh, god, what, what can I say? What words
can I go to? I can't keep quiet any more!

ELECTRA
What is the matter? What makes you say that?

ORESTES
Am I in the noble presence of Electra?

ELECTRA
Yes, but you find it in a miserable condition.

ORESTES
So much sadness, even though I find you here.

ELECTRA
Surely, sir, you are not grieving for my sake.

ORESTES
Poor thing, profaned, blasphemously ruined!   1140

ELECTRA
Sir, you speak of the ill fortune that is mine.

ORESTES
The pity of it, oh, your sad, unmarried life!

ELECTRA

Stranger, why should you stare at me and grieve?

ORESTES

I have been aware of so few of my own sorrows.

ELECTRA

What have we said here that makes you see that?

ORESTES

Seeing how many injuries you've endured.

ELECTRA

What you can see, though, are only a few of them.

ORESTES

How could there be any worse than these?

ELECTRA

I am compelled to live with the murderers.

ORESTES

Whose murderers? What evils are you talking about?   1150

ELECTRA

My father's. And they have made me their slave.

ORESTES

And who has put this harsh constraint on you?

ELECTRA

By name, my mother; by actions, something else.

ORESTES

What actions? Hard hands, or hard restrictions?

ELECTRA

Violence, punishment, any wickedness at all.

ORESTES

There is no one to help you or protect you?

ELECTRA

No. You have shown me my one protector's ashes.

ORESTES

Poor woman, looking at you makes me pity you.

ELECTRA

Well, you are the first to take pity on me.

ORESTES

Yes, I am the only one to share your suffering.   1160

ELECTRA

Surely you are not some distant relative.

ORESTES

I can say, if these women are trustworthy.

ELECTRA

They are; you may speak safely before them.

ORESTES

Give back the urn, then, and hear everything.

ELECTRA

No, no, for gods' sake, sir, don't do that!

ORESTES

Look, there is no risk in doing what I say.

ELECTRA

No, I beg you by your beard, don't take what I love most!

ORESTES

You must not keep it.

ELECTRA

The ultimate agony,

Orestes, if I cannot bury you!

ORESTES

Don't say that! There is no reason to mourn!   1170

ELECTRA

No reason to mourn my brother's death?

ORESTES

It is not right to speak of him that way.

ELECTRA

So you refuse me my rights in the dead man?

ORESTES

You are denied nothing, but there are no such rights.

ELECTRA

There are if this is the body of Orestes.

ORESTES

This is not he, except as words have made him so.

ELECTRA

Then where is the tomb of that unlucky man?

ORESTES

Nowhere; a living man has no need of a tomb.

ELECTRA
Young man, what are you saying?

ORESTES
                                    Not one false word.

ELECTRA
You say he is alive?

ORESTES
                                    He is if I am.   1180

ELECTRA
How? Are you the man?

ORESTES
                              Look at this signet
that was my father's. You see? It is the truth.

ELECTRA
O dawning light, O love . . .

ORESTES
                                    Love, I see it too.

ELECTRA
O voice, are you here?

ORESTES
                              Do not ask of another.

ELECTRA
Is it you I am holding in my arms?

ORESTES
                                    As always.

ELECTRA

    Dearest friends, women of this town, you see
    Orestes, first by a contrivance killed,
    by new contrivance brought home alive and safe.

CHORUS

    Daughter, we behold him. Your good fortune
    brings tears of rejoicing to our eyes.   1190

ELECTRA

    Oh, child,
    child, body dearest to me,
    you have come home, found,
    arrived, and seen those you longed for.

ORESTES

    Here I am. Be quiet now, and wait.

ELECTRA

    What is it?

ORESTES

    Better not let them hear inside. Stay quiet.

ELECTRA

    I swear by the spirit of Artemis,
    eternal virgin, never to fear
    the women who stay in the palace.   1200
    They are a useless weight on the earth.

ORESTES

    Remember, women can burn with the war-god's fire;
    I think you know this from experience.

ELECTRA

Oh, god, god.
You remind me of the way our griefs began,
cloudy and vague, never
to be undone, never forgotten.

ORESTES

I know that, too. But wait for the right moment
before we take the time to remember these things.

ELECTRA

All of time, every moment, would be the one   1210
to speak. I have just had my lips set free.

ORESTES

I understand you, but your freedom needs protection.

ELECTRA

What should I do?

ORESTES

For now, do not talk too much. Now is not the time.

ELECTRA

But what good is silence when there are words
to say that you are here, that I can look at you,
as I had not lately thought or hoped to do?

ORESTES

I did not come until I was moved by the gods
and with their help had done what I have done.

ELECTRA

It would be a grace   1220
even higher than the first, if a god
is what has brought you home. Divine force,
I believe, has made it happen.

ORESTES

    I do not want to restrain your happiness,
    but your joyful noise makes me nervous.

ELECTRA

    O you, O time—
    how long you waited to take
    this happiest journey home to me.
    You see me in my suffering. Do not—

ORESTES

    Do not?   1230

ELECTRA

    Do not stop me from touching your face.

ORESTES

    I would be angry to see someone else do it.

ELECTRA

    May I?

ORESTES

    Of course.

ELECTRA

    Oh, love, I heard
    a voice I thought I would not hear again,
    and still I controlled my feelings,
    and kept silence as I listened.
    But I have you here now, before me,
    the whole look of you,   1240
    that I can't forget even in the worst of times.

ORESTES

    For now, leave out the useless words. No need
    to let me know how evil our mother is,

or how fast our father's estate is dwindling
because of Aegisthus and his spendthrift ways.
More talking only complicates our timing.
What I need to know now is how things are,
what the best way is for us to proceed,
whether to break in, where to hide and wait—
how to carry out our mission and silence   1250
the laughter of our enemies. Make sure
our mother doesn't see the joy in your eyes
when we go inside. Keep up the grieving,
as if our false catastrophe were genuine.
After the job is finished and we have won,
we'll be free to laugh a little ourselves.

ELECTRA

My dear, whatever you want is what I want,
since all my joy comes from you. It's not my own.
I wouldn't cause you the slightest pain
in return for even the greatest benefit.   1260
That would insult the god who rules this moment.
Now then. Of course you know how things are here.
You have been told that Aegisthus is away
and that my mother is at home. Forget about
the risk that she will ever see me smiling;
my hatred for her is fastened to my soul,
and now that I've seen you, the tears of joy
won't stop flowing from my eyes. How could they?
In one arrival you have been both dead
and living. Do you know what you have done?   1270
It is beyond understanding; if my father
were to walk in here alive, I would not think
it was an apparition; I would know him
for himself. You have come the same way,
and I will do whatever you ask me to.
If I had been left alone, my only choice
would have been between an honorable death
and, if possible, honorable survival.

ORESTES
   Quiet. Someone is coming out the door.

ELECTRA
   Strangers, go in, for what you have with you   1280
   no one would turn away—or be happy to have.
(Enter the Paedogogus.)

PAEDOGOGUS
   Idiots! Have you lost your minds? Are you tired
   of living? Did you ever have any sense?
   You are not merely at the brink, you're deep
   in the middle of very serious danger!
   If I had not been standing by these doors,
   your plans would have preceded your corpses inside.
   But I have looked out for you this time.
   Now cut out the long speeches and the joyful shouts
   with which you are so well supplied, and go.   1290
   Inside. Hesitation now is dangerous,
   and the time has come to get it over with.

ORESTES
   Tell me what the situation is inside.

PAEDOGOGUS
   Excellent. I've made sure no one will know you.

ORESTES
   I suppose you've informed them that I am dead.

PAEDOGOGUS
   As far as they're concerned you're with the ghosts.

ORESTES
   Are they glad to hear it? What are they saying?

PAEDOGOGUS
I'll go into that when we're all done here.
For now, all is well; even their troubles assist us.

ELECTRA
Orestes, who is this man, in god's name?   1300

ORESTES
Don't you know him?

ELECTRA
                                        No! I can't imagine who he is!

ORESTES
You don't know the hands you gave me to?

ELECTRA
What man? What do you mean?

ORESTES
                                                    I mean the man
whose hand you chose to guide me away to Phocis.

ELECTRA
Him? The one man I found I could trust
that awful day our father was murdered?

ORESTES
This is he! No more of this inquisition!

ELECTRA
O dawning light, O lone savior of the house
of Agamemnon, how did you get here?
Are you the one who rescued me and my brother   1310
from so many dangers? O hands that I love,

O dearest feet, how could you be here so long
and stay unknown to me and keep your counsel?
You said murderous, maddening things, yet did
the things I longed for most. Welcome, father,
as I think I see a father in you, welcome,
and know this: in one day I have hated you
and loved you as I have no other man.

PAEDOGOGUS

    I think that will do for now. As for the tale
    of what has been, there are days and nights ahead,   1320
    Electra, when all that will be clear to you.
    Now, listen. Here we are, here is the time,
    since Clytemnestra is alone inside,
    no soldiers near her. If you hesitate,
    they will be back, and you will have to fight
    with them and even stronger reinforcements.

ORESTES

    Pylades, our mission needs no more speeches.
    We'll go in now, asking as we go for blessing
    from my father's gods, the guardians of these gates.
(Orestes and Pylades enter the palace, followed by the Paedogogus and
               their two attendants. Electra remains outside and
               addresses the statue.)

ELECTRA

    Lord Apollo, hear them, and hear me!   1330
    Many times I have stood in prayer before you,
    making such offerings as I had. And now again,
    Lycian Apollo, with what I have I beg,
    I fall down before you and implore,
    bless and guide these plans of ours, and show
    the world what mortals may receive from gods
    in return for their mortal transgressions.
(Electra goes into the palace.)

CHORUS
    Behold. The god of strife
    strides on, and breathes blood-vengeance.
    On the track of evil crimes, the hounds   1340
    have gone into the palace
    and will hunt their quarry down.
    It will not be long
    that the dream within me hangs unfulfilled.
    On stealthy feet the avenger
    of the dead enters the house of his fathers
    and its ancient riches,
    and the blood on his hands
    is a weapon whetted toward another act of blood.
    And Maia's son, Hermes, is quick   1350
    to lead through the dark that hid this plot.
(Enter Electra from the palace.)

ELECTRA
    Dearest women, the men will finish their work
    at any moment now. Let us wait quietly.

CHORUS
    What, then? What are they doing?

ELECTRA
                                   She is preparing the urn
    for burial, and those two are close upon her.

CHORUS
    Why did you come out so quickly?

ELECTRA
                                   To stand watch
    and keep Aegisthus from surprising us.

CLYTEMNESTRA *(heard from inside the palace)*
Oh, god! No friends here!
Murderers in the house!

ELECTRA
Someone inside is screaming. Can you hear, my dears?   1360

CHORUS
What I heard
was terrifying. I am shivering.

CLYTEMNESTRA *(heard from inside the palace)*
Oh, god! Aegisthus! Where, where are you?

ELECTRA
Again! Hear that? Someone screaming!

CLYTEMNESTRA *(heard from inside the palace)*
Oh, son, my baby,
pity your mother!

ELECTRA
You never pitied him,
or the father who sired him!

CHORUS
O city! O miserable clan, now
one more, one more sunset in your round of days!

CLYTEMNESTRA *(heard from inside the palace)*
Aaah! Stabbed!

ELECTRA
Stab again, twice as hard, if you can!

CLYTEMNESTRA *(heard from inside the palace)*
    Aaah! Again!

ELECTRA

                                Good! I wish it were Aegisthus too!   1370

CHORUS
    The old curses have come home!
    From under the ground
    the dead rise up and spill the blood
    of those who murdered them in the old days!
(Enter Orestes and Pylades from the palace.)
    Look, here they are! A bloody sacrifice
    to the god of strife drips from a red hand
    that I cannot blame.

ELECTRA
    Orestes, are you—?

ORESTES

                                All is well
    in the palace if Apollo's prophecy was good.

ELECTRA
    Is the bitch dead?

ORESTES

                                Never fear again   1380
    the insults of your mother's evil pride.

CHORUS
    Wait, stop. I can see
    Aegisthus off there, approaching.

ELECTRA
    Back, boys!

ORESTES

Where do you see him?

ELECTRA

Coming in from the edge of town,
smiling like a man who has heard good news.

CHORUS

Get back inside from the entrance, quick, now,
so you can do this job as you did the last one.

ORESTES

Courage. We'll do it.

ELECTRA

Hurry! Go where you have to go!

ORESTES

Yes. I'm gone.

ELECTRA

I will handle things here.   1390
(Orestes and Pylades go back into the palace.)

CHORUS

It would be good to say a few kind words
to him, so he will not suspect
the trap justice has set for him.
(Enter Aegisthus.)

AEGISTHUS

Which of you knows where the men from Phocis are,
who came here, they say, with word that Orestes
has been killed in a chariot-racing accident?
You: yes, I ask you, who used to be so bold,
because I think you cared the most for him
and therefore have the greatest need to know.

ELECTRA

    I know it quite well, of course. Otherwise   1400
    I would be ignorant of the ills of those I love.

AEGISTHUS

    Where are the strangers, then? Speak up!

ELECTRA

    Inside. They have charmed their hostess.

AEGISTHUS

    Have they really reported that he is dead?

ELECTRA

    Not just reported. They brought certain proof.

AEGISTHUS

    Is it something we can see and recognize?

ELECTRA

    Yes, it is, and there are fairer sights.

AEGISTHUS

    I rarely take such pleasure in your speech.

ELECTRA

    You are welcome to what pleasure you may find.

AEGISTHUS

    I command you all to be silent now, and open up   1410
    the gates so all Argives and Mycenaeans
    may see inside. Anyone who might have been
    inspired by false hopes of this man may see
    his corpse, then calmly take the bit from my hand,
    and need no force from me to learn good sense.

ELECTRA

    I, for one, will do what is required.
    I have learned in time who is most powerful.
(The doors of the palace are swung open. Orestes and Pylades stand
              beside a covered bier.)

AEGISTHUS

    O Zeus, this thing I see, the wrath of gods
    destroyed, and yet if I am angry, let
    that go unsaid. Undo the coverings   1420
    over the face and let me grieve my relative.

ORESTES

    Undo them yourself. This moment is not mine
    but yours, to see this and speak loving words.

AEGISTHUS

    I will take your good advice.
(to Electra)
                      But you
    call Clytemnestra, if she is in the palace.

ORESTES

    She is close by. No need to search the palace.
(Aegisthus lifts the covering.)

AEGISTHUS

    Aaah! What do I see?

ORESTES

                 What frightens you? A stranger's face?

AEGISTHUS

    Who are these men whose trap I failed to see?

ORESTES

Do you see now that you, a living man,
have been talking to men you thought were dead?   1430

AEGISTHUS

I get your riddle. It can only be
that this is Orestes who is speaking.

ORESTES

Ah. Such a prophet. Yet were you fooled just now?

AEGISTHUS

It's over, I am doomed. But let me speak
just a brief word.

ELECTRA

                                        Do not let him speak,
brother, do not give him time for last words!
If a man is caught up in misfortune,
doomed to die, what good is a little time?
No. Kill him now, and throw his body out
for creatures who know how to bury his kind,   1440
far out of sight. This is the only way
to free me from the weight of ancient crimes.

ORESTES *(to Aegisthus)*

Go in now. This is mortal combat, not debate.

AEGISTHUS

Why should I go inside? If this is just,
why hide it instead of killing me right here?

ORESTES

No commands from you. Go where my father died,
and there we'll find a place for you to die.

AEGISTHUS

    Is this house doomed to witness every one
    of the curses visited on Pelops' line?

ORESTES

    It is doomed to witness yours, in any case;   1450
    my prophecies are skillful in this matter.

AEGISTHUS

    This skill you brag about was not your father's.

ORESTES

    You will talk on. No more delays; go in.

AEGISTHUS

    You lead the way.

ORESTES

                No, you go first.

AEGISTHUS

                        So I won't get away?

ORESTES

    No, so you won't get to choose where you die.
    I'll see to it that your death is bitter pain.
    Such punishment should justly come to all
    who carry on their lives outside the law.
    Kill them all! There would be fewer scoundrels.
(Aegisthus, followed by Orestes and Pylades, goes into the palace.)

CHORUS

    O seed of Atreus, after such time   1460
    of suffering, you have come at last to freedom
    and completion in the struggles of this day.

Philoctetes

Translated by
Armand Schwerner

Translator's Preface

How to have them say what they must?

You have to con Philoctetes. Use the language. (42)

If he sees me and has his bow with him I'm dead,
and so are you, because of me . . . (61–62)

                             . . . you shrink
from the music of deceit. (64–65)

                  If *you* fail, *we* fail.
Troy will elude us, the Greeks will grieve,
we must have this man's bow. (54–57)

The translator looks again at his adventures in the latitudes of speech-modes. Reasonably colloquial, intermittently hieratic. As in any transmission, to enter into the work, the body, and re-make. What can help? Historical perspective, some understanding of class structure, an attempt to inform the translation with an appreciation of the differences between the assumptions of fifth-century B.C. Athens and those of our own time . . . And what remains is almost everything. These powerful, aristocratic men, power-lust and righteousness, and nevertheless the subtly pervasive harmonics of *moira*, *ananke*. And pain, a lot of pain.

When an unbearable hurt comes, the words, the rhetoric, go:

$$\pi\alpha\pi\alpha\hat{\iota},$$
$$\dot{\alpha}\pi\alpha\pi\pi\alpha\pi\alpha\hat{\iota}, \pi\alpha\pi\alpha\pi\pi\alpha\pi\alpha\pi\pi\alpha\pi\alpha\pi\pi\alpha\pi\alpha\hat{\iota} \text{ (Loeb, 745–46)}$$

which is near the extreme point on the continuum; from that wrenched cry to the lyricism and compassionate clarity of the Chorus:

$$\overset{.}{\Upsilon}\pi\nu' \,\dot{o}\delta\acute{v}\nu\alpha\varsigma, \,\dot{\alpha}\delta\alpha\acute{\eta}\varsigma, \,\overset{..}{\Upsilon}\pi\nu\epsilon \,\delta' \,\dot{\alpha}\lambda\gamma\acute{\epsilon}\omega\nu,$$
$$\epsilon\dot{v}\alpha\grave{\epsilon}\varsigma \,\dot{\eta}\mu\hat{\iota}\nu \,\overset{'}{\epsilon}\lambda\theta\iota\varsigma,$$

εὐαίων, εὐαίων, ὦναξ.
ὄμμασι δ' ἀντίοχοις
τάνδ' αἴγλαν, ἃ τέταται τανῦν.
ἴθι ἴθι μοι παιών. (827–32)

The translator, carrier-over, owes the play-language and himself an immersion in the extensive field of those possibilities. Faithfulness to the tone. If in doubt, cut. But why still another translation of *Philoctetes*? The Loeb edition of the Greek text (1913) presents the following translation:

> Sleep immune of cares,
> Sleep that knows not cumber,
> Breathe thy softest airs,
> Prince of painless slumber!
> O'er his eyes always
> Let thy dream-light play;
> Healer come, we pray.

Ababccc, not too reasonably, the text giving abcbda. The real problem here lies in the fact that, as Robert Fitzgerald has pointed out, "Rhyme as we know it was unknown to Greek poetry." In any case, seven lines for six. What is the compulsion for this kind of ordering?

Thomas Francklin (1938) gives:

> Sleep, thou patron of mankind,
> Great physician of the mind,
> Who dost nor pain nor sorrow know,
> Sweetest balm of every woe,
> Mildest sovereign, hear us now;
> Hear thy wretched suppliant's vow;
> His eyes in gentle slumbers close,
> And continue his repose;
> Hear the wretched suppliant's vow,
> Great physician, hear us now.

Aabbccddee; four-stress couplets, arbitrarily; almost metronomic; ten lines for six; the deadly language of "poetry" in a sterile version of eighteenth-century modes. When in doubt, add? Enforce symmetry?

David Grene (1957) renders the Greek lines as follows:

> Sleep that knows not pain nor suffering
> Kindly upon us, Lord,
> Kindly, kindly come.
> Spread your enveloping radiance,
> As now, over his eyes.
> Come, come, Lord Healer.

Six lines for six; marked by skillful restraint; a significant lyrical movement, but still bearing the continuing afflictions of syntactical inversion and archaic diction; some overdependence on repetition and a kind of "august" stage language to heighten reader response: "knows not . . . nor," "kindly come," and so on.

In the present version the lines read:

> Lord Sleep, breathe
> a quiet music for him.
> Lord of peace not pain,
> flow in your calm over his eyes. Come
> lord healer, come. (650–54)

Is it "better"? In any case it does represent the effort to work in pretty straight conversational syntax, to minimize interruptive punctuation in the interest of flow, to commonly de-emphasize phrasal and clausal webs.

Can this tragedy work on the stage today and tomorrow, in the context of good plays working through the complex presence of our American? I wanted very much to produce a translation whose language has a playable vivacity—a version essentially faithful to the original, but subject to my sense of pace and rhythm in the language we speak. For instance, I felt the need to cut through what I experienced as the prolixity of stichomythia, the full-sentence formalities of line-for-line conversations. I hope I have succeeded in rendering the force and sharpness of many colloquies without calling on the rhetoric or implicit worldview of naturalistic theater.

The various dramatic embodiments of subtle and shifting psychological states—which talk to us with such extraordinary presence—evoke in us constant recognition. We may summarize very briefly the essentials of the plot. Philoctetes, through no fault of his own, is brought low; he didn't know he had breached a sacred precinct, where he was bitten in the foot by a venomous snake. The wound, which gave off a dreadful stench, never healed, and his fellow Greeks exiled him to the island of Lemnos, the site of the play's action. The very Greeks who had isolated him return in order to bring him back to assist in the overthrow of Troy: Philoctetes owns the bow of Heracles, which never misses. Oracular word has come that Philoctetes and the bow are essential to winning the war. Wily Odysseus, originally responsible for subtracting Philoctetes from his fellow Greeks, is accompanied on his second visit to Lemnos by the young Neoptolemus, appointed as the seducer through whom Greece will overcome Philoctetes' anger and refusals. Much of the play presents the complex interactions between the wounded man and Odysseus' young associate. Neoptolemus, moved by the exile's plight, gives him back the magic bow, but before Heracles enters into the action Philoctetes still refuses to return home.

Heracles, the god-from-the-machine, appears suddenly at the end of the play to insist on Philoctetes' submission. A vast shadow separates the god's utterance and the exile's experience. The contemporary reader may experience an almost uncanny sense of category error. But the god in his dictates works a power. It is in the conjunction of two orders: Philoctetes' and Neoptolemus' moral and psychological growth in self-awareness and the matrix of the Necessity to which they must submit.

And yet, and yet . . . Obeisance paid to that Necessity, *Ananke*, we, being who we are, tend to set aside our dutiful recognitions. The state of the twentieth-century person's *polis* exacerbates his or her wanderings in the trammels of the Western primacies of *self-development* and *individuation*, or worse, *rugged individualism*—god-words. Shared submission? Shared order? In our heterogeneous republic *E pluribus unum* is common currency— on coins.

Partly Romanticism's egregious spawn, the hideous *Volk*-appeals and acts of too many Reichs have inoculated many of us against the desirable benignities of oneness; these unfortunately share the world stage with fundamentalism's despair and acting-out, or worse. The modern temper throws up the twin infirmities of Western individualism and Third World absolutism. The Greeks had a word for the world: *oikoumene, the* world, theirs, as opposed to the barbarians' turf. They also had a word—*idiote*—for the citizen who by shirking communal responsibility violated the city-state.

In the West legal oversight is hard put to keep up with the illegal schemes of financial adventurers. In Afghanistan the God-intoxicated young men of the Taliban will not permit women to work, allowing only the women's eyes to be seen publicly on pain of being beaten on the street by the young acolytes of God-patrols. There burglars' offenses cost them their hands; neighbors stone adulterers. Once anthropology's presentations of alien curiosities, such fundamentalist pleasures now count as commercially vectored nodes on the rhizome of world television. Such pleasures are book-ends to advertising's skilled manipulation of graphic and literary techniques and its fawning praise of the Western celebrities they half-create.

How do the applications of pervasive well-paid advertising skills, practiced by well-educated people in "creative" departments, affect our relationship to the function and meaning of language, to the referents of language? We ponder the difference—so hard to conceive, to come toward sensately—between the life-in-language of fifth-century Athens and ours.

For the reader of *Philoctetes* the inescapable, invasive paraphernalia of world commerce symbolize the modern master problem of the nature of the sacred and the manner of its expression and appearance, its very existence—how are we to experience Attic tragedies? It is in response to our endless wobble that we keep retranslating the tragedies, continue to seek new values in our theatrical productions. So, for instance, like the imaginative director Andrei Serban we produce versions in language-mixes or invented tongues, all the while hoping that our audiences can find some new-old connections to ancient ritual plots and their seductive hieratic mantras.

The come-and-go Jack-in-the-box acts of daily world news are the great delusive narrative cycle of the planet, hungry daily for its paparazzi-feed and entropic thrills. Television soap opera renders the illusion of new excitement while furnishing the security of the unchallengingly predictable in the service of the mercantile. Much present journalism—both print and electronic—approaches the powerful delusive condition of soap opera. A ubiquitous *Dallas*, say, feeds the appetites of billions in the People's Republic of China and elsewhere around the planet; its glossily shallow inanities, redolent of American power, add to the lingua franca of the world's crypto-mythologies. What is the name of the sacred?

The semiologist, descriptive and analytical, professionally uninterested in value-making distinctions between Heracles and Spiderman, is the instructive homogenizer of postmodernism. Viewed in such light, the idea of the sacred is an evanescent spume downed between the clicks of the television remote or awash in the interstices among John Cage's aleatoric cadences. Some artists, on soteriological alert, conceive of that very process—artistic method based on randomized sampling—as the sacred as they feel the need to redefine the relationship between intention/consciousness and poetry. Anti-Prometheans, we have pulled down the powers of randomness from the Empyrean, achieving one of the supreme post-Renaissance domestications.

So we are not surprised that the dialogical directness of *Philoctetes* supports a twentieth-century reader's sense of its apparent foregrounding of individual psychology and the anguishing power of individual responsibility and decision making exercised against a blank sky. Scholars have often emphasized the degree to which *Philoctetes*' dialogue-language is closer to conversational Greek than is that of any other Greek tragedy. The presence of the gods and the mystery of necessity, however acknowledged, can easily seem to the modern reader a "diminished thing." Consider a contemporary American's puzzlement at Philoctetes' punishment, not the nature of his servitude but that he should have been found guilty in the first place. In Kafka's *The Trial* Joseph K. is accused of . . . guilt. But that novel is a comic and metaphysical conundrum, not an embodiment of cultural values.

It is hard to know how much a contemporary American can read into Philoctetes' penultimate utterance, which may appear less as evidence of willing submission to the divine than as a moan of satisfaction and gratitude: he is being taken back home. Philoctetes' submission, deeply grounded in place, home, will in two millennia yield to Heidegger's sense of the pervasive, near-universal loss of *heimat*, home-ness.

Philoctetes will return, finally, after incredible suffering and courage, but this compelling figure who moved us so by the exercise of his staunch, defying will is left behind, grounded forever on his island prison. Another Philoctetes returns home. By allowing Neoptolemus to convey him back to Greece and the hated Greeks who had so wronged him, the wounded protagonist's terminal utterance to Heracles breaks our hearts. Philoctetes forever bequeaths the agony of his valiant and tortured self to the island ground he had come through his suffering to love, and now must leave. His gift of self through the agency of Heracles relates perhaps not so much to right or wrong or to the bizarreries of divine justice as to the grittier pull of the land of Greece, his first place:

> ὦ φθέγμα ποθεινὸν ἐμοὶ πέμψας
> χρόνιός τε φανείς,
> οὐκ ἀπιθήσω τοῖς σοῖς μύθοις. (Loeb, 1445–47)

> I've longed so long for your voice,
> your form returns after such losses,
> I will not disobey you. (1188–90)

Cast

ODYSSEUS
NEOPTOLEMUS, son of Achilles, prince of Scyros
CHORUS of sailor companions of Odysseus and Neoptolemus
PHILOCTETES, son of Poeas
SAILOR (disguised as a captain)
HERACLES
NONSPEAKING
    Assistant
    Second sailor

*(The play occurs in a lonely place on Lemnos island, in front of a
cliff showing the entrance to Philoctetes' cave. Odysseus and
Neoptolemus enter, accompanied by an assistant.)*

ODYSSEUS
    Finally, Lemnos island, see how dreary
    this place, no people, no houses,
    nothing and no one
    except Philoctetes, Poeas' son.

                                    Neoptolemus,
    you're the son of our shining father Achilles,
    let me make it absolutely clear, I left Philoctetes here
    on the prince's orders: it was unbearable,
    his rotting foot and its pus, his screams and moans
    unnerving everyone, souring our rites and our sacrifices.

    Well, no point going on about it. There's no time.   10
    If he finds me here I'll never be able to take him back.
    I need your help, take a look around, we're looking
    for a cave with a double entrance. It'll have one alcove
    the sun warms in winter, in the other
    cool breezes dissipate the heat.

Over to the left a little you'll see a fountain
where he drinks, if he's alive. If you see anything,
signal, then we'll talk further.

NEOPTOLEMUS
I think I see it. A cave.

ODYSSEUS
Where? Up or down?   20

NEOPTOLEMUS
Up there. But there's no sign of a path.

ODYSSEUS
Maybe he's lying down. Have a look.

NEOPTOLEMUS
Nobody.

ODYSSEUS
No food? How about utensils? Anything?

NEOPTOLEMUS
Just a bed of leaves.

ODYSSEUS
And?

NEOPTOLEMUS
A wooden bowl. Pretty crude. Some kindling.

ODYSSEUS
His whole treasure . . .

NEOPTOLEMUS
Here are some rags, drying, grayish-yellow with pus.

ODYSSEUS

> This must be his place. He's probably nearby   30
> with that bad leg, out to find food I suppose,
> or medicinal herbs. Set a watch on him.
> He's one man I'd rather not be surprised by.
> He'd rather take me than any Greek alive.

(Assistant leaves.)

NEOPTOLEMUS

> I'll arrange for the guard. Now
> go on. You have more to say.

ODYSSEUS

> Son of Achilles, today you must prove
> who you are, and not just with your body.
> I'm setting you a task, strange to you, but you must
> do it. You came to serve.   40

NEOPTOLEMUS

> What do I do?

ODYSSEUS

> You have to con Philoctetes. Use the language.
> When he asks you about yourself, tell him
> "Achilles' son." No need to lie about that. But
> tell him more, that you're sailing home in anger,
> having left the fleet in anger.
> The Greek chiefs lied to you and betrayed you.
> To take Troy they had to have you, seduced you
> into leaving home, and when you joined them
> they ripped you away from Achilles' weapons, your father's   50
> weapons, that you had a right to, and gave them
> to Odysseus, gave those arms to Odysseus.
> When you say my name, curse me, spit on Odysseus.
> That's no pain for me: if *you* fail, *we* fail.
> Troy will elude us, the Greeks will grieve,
> we must have this man's bow.

I'll explain why you can meet him and why I can't.
You're here freely, not bound by a pledge or an oath.
Nor did you belong to the first fleet.
But I *am* bound, and I *was* present. That's it.   60
If he sees me and has his bow with him, I'm dead,
and so are you, because of me.
Can you deliver that unconquered bow? I know
the dishonesty sickens you, you shrink
from the music of deceit. But winning is sweet,
today is for courage, tomorrow for honesty; be mine
for one hour of lies; as to the rest, your probity,
the endless future will bear witness.

NEOPTOLEMUS
Son of Laertes, what I hate to hear, what rasps
my ears, I hate to do. That's how I am. I loathe the smell   70
of deceit, and they tell me my father did too. I am ready
to deliver Philoctetes. By force. I won't by fraud.
He can't withstand us, crippled as he is. Prince,
since I am sent to help you
I'm worried about seeming passive, but
I'd rather fail with honor than sink
into victory.

ODYSSEUS
Son of great Achilles, when I was young
I bound my tongue and winged my hand, like you.
But our common pain has taught me   80
the tongue's ultimate power.

NEOPTOLEMUS
You want me to lie.

ODYSSEUS
To snare Philoctetes.

NEOPTOLEMUS
   And not persuade him? Deceive him?

ODYSSEUS
   Persuasion's as useless as force.

NEOPTOLEMUS
   Why are his weapons so incredible?

ODYSSEUS
   They never miss. Death comes immediately.

NEOPTOLEMUS
   But if a brave man . . .

ODYSSEUS
   No. Only stratagems will work. I told you that.

NEOPTOLEMUS
   Lies don't shame you?   90

ODYSSEUS
   Not if success depends on them.

NEOPTOLEMUS
   An adult is responsible for his face
   How can he confront the world if . . . ?

ODYSSEUS
   If you have qualms you lose.

NEOPTOLEMUS
   How do I profit if we do get him to Troy?

ODYSSEUS
    Without the bow we can't sack Troy.

NEOPTOLEMUS
    You said *I* would take the town.

ODYSSEUS
    You and the bow; the bow not without you.

NEOPTOLEMUS
    In that case the quarry's worth going after.

ODYSSEUS
    If you make it you win twice.   100

NEOPTOLEMUS
    Make that clear and I'll try.

ODYSSEUS
    They'll call you brave; but they'll also say: "a wise man."

NEOPTOLEMUS
    I'll throw out my shame and do it.

ODYSSEUS
    You remember my instructions?

NEOPTOLEMUS
    Enough; I said I'd do it; I'll do it.

ODYSSEUS
    Stay here then; wait till he comes.
    I don't want to be seen so I'll go
    and bring the guard back to the ship with me.
    If you stay away for long, he'll come back
    disguised as a sailor. You won't know him,   110

so be alert. Listen carefully, his cryptic words
will cloak his message. It's up to you now
and back to the ship for me.
Hermes,
god of cunning,
be with us.
Athena, mistress of victory, goddess
of the City, who has never failed me,
support us now.
(Exit Odysseus; enter Chorus.)

CHORUS

Sir, we're strangers in this strange place, how   120
will we talk and what should we hide?
How should we act with the man we're looking for?
Let us know: you have a special power of perception
handed you from Zeus; you hold the scepter.
And the skill is yours from your father's father's fathers.
Young lord, what can we do?

NEOPTOLEMUS

If you want to find his hiding place, go on.
When you see the wanderer come back, leave
his cave and come back too. I may need you.

CHORUS

We will do what we've done and will go on doing,   130
care for you.
Now we should know
where he lives and rests, we must be on guard
and watch for an attack. Where does he walk?
Is he at home?

NEOPTOLEMUS *(walks toward the cave)*
There's the double door of his cave
and there's the inner rock he uses for a bed.

CHORUS
    Where is the poor man?

NEOPTOLEMUS
    Probably out looking for food.
    His wound never heals, and goes on hurting.   140
    So he limps around, stumbling
    on game, his arrows between him and famine.

CHORUS
    Poor man, forgotten by every man, how we pity him,
    plagued by his disease and the absence of love.
    How can he stand the endless aloneness?
    A man shudders his way to death and the path is pain.
    In spite of his lineage he's bereft
    and endures his hunger and incurable wound
    with only wild and spotted beast for company,
    except for the blabbing of far away echo   150
    that returns his bitter cries to him.

NEOPTOLEMUS
    His pain's no accident,
    sent I think by pitiless Chryse.
    There's a design to what distresses him:
    a wise god knew about the war before the war began,
    knows now the harsh
    minute of Troy's death, and fixes the song
    of Philoctetes' marvelous bow
    to the one hour where his absolute arrows
    will realize for Troy the promise of its end.   160

CHORUS
    Shh.

NEOPTOLEMUS
    Why?
(Philoctetes approaches slowly, limping.)

CHORUS
   Listen. A man, limping? It is here?
   Here? It's getting nearer now, clear
   sound of groping feet, and now still far
   but nearing, distinctly, a voice of pain.
   Get ready, prince.

NEOPTOLEMUS
   For what?

CHORUS
   New trouble. He's closer. He's no shepherd
   and that sound's no syrinx melody.   170
   Just listen to the harsh cries, born maybe
   from his stumbles on the wounding road. Or is he still, eyes
   clearly fixed on the cold port,
   his trial one with the inhospitable sea.
(Enter Philoctetes, limping.)

PHILOCTETES
   You, strangers,
   who are you, your stock, from where,
   ending up here on this island
   of depression and refusals? Your clothes, the way
   you look, you must be Greeks. You make my eyes
   happy; talk to me, let me hear you talk.   180
   If I look strange to you let it be.
   I have no friends; I'm alone; I'm stranded here;
   pity me. If you're here as friends, I beg you,
   talk to me as I do to you.

NEOPTOLEMUS
   Your first question: we're Greeks, you're right.

PHILOCTETES
   Wonderful, how wonderful to hear Greek again.
   What quest brought you? The wind

that ordered your sails was a happy wind.
Tell me everything. I want to know my friend.

NEOPTOLEMUS

I'm from Scyros, where the waves lap the coast,   190
and I'm going home. My name is Neoptolemus.
My father's Achilles. You know everything now.

PHILOCTETES

Son of a dear father,
son of a very dear land,
foster-son of old Lycomedes, what
do you need here? What port did you sail from?

NEOPTOLEMUS

I sailed straight from Ilium.

PHILOCTETES

Ilium? Is it . . . Could you . . . Were you on board
when our fleet first sailed for Troy?

NEOPTOLEMUS

What do you mean? Were you there?   200

PHILOCTETES

O my son, you don't know who you're talking to?

NEOPTOLEMUS

Should I know a complete stranger?

PHILOCTETES

Not even my name? You don't know
even my name? They never told you
the growing rot in my body?

NEOPTOLEMUS

I don't know anything about all this.

PHILOCTETES

    Oh, the gods forsake me, not one word
    of my misery has reached home.
    But the jackals who marooned me laugh, keep
    quiet, my wound keeps hurting   210
    and gets worse every day.
    O my boy, Achilles' son, you never heard
    about that man, me, Philoctetes, son of Poeas,
    inheritor of Heracles' bow, me, thrown
    out by the Atridae and the Cephallenian prince,
    me, wasted, a tramp, struck by plague, chosen
    for death through the hollow envenoming tooth
    of a man-killer snake.
    That's how they left me, plagued.
    Exhausted from tossing sleeplessness, I'd fallen   220
    into sleep under a beachrock and they laughed
    at my state as they left for the ships.
    They donated some used rags, a beggar's alms,
    and table leftovers, may the gods
    lay them this low one day soon.
    Picture, my son: I wake,
    all men gone, what a waking, tears
    and distraught cries when I see the ships that had borne me
    sailed from my life, no man left to share
    the absences or care for me and my hurt.   230
    I looked everywhere, my son, and found pain, nothing
    else as the days and months grew years. I cared
    for myself under this sad roof. When hunger came
    I shot doves and crawled to retrieve what my taut
    bowstring and my arrow had delivered, and all the time
    my wasted foot kept dragging heavily on the ground.
    If I needed water, if I had to have firewood,
    when winter frosted the ground, I'd get them. No fire
    except for hard rock flint on flint, the hidden spark
    that keeps me alive. The bare roof and the fire's all I need.   240
    Except for the healing of my hurt.
    Now my son, about this island:

No sailor *wants* to sail here: no anchorage, no
market for goods and profit, no place to sleep and eat.
Prudent men stay away. The rare accidental visitors
give me pity, food, or clothes.
But when I talk of home they leave alone.
So it's ten years now for me, lingering on,
hungry, dying piece by piece.
Only the worm that gnaws me flourishes.   250
My son, I owe this misery to the Atridae and Odysseus.
May the gods lay them this low one day soon.

CHORUS

O son of Poeas, as much as those visitors I pity you.

NEOPTOLEMUS

I'm witness to the truth of your story.
I've lived with the evil of the Atridae and of Odysseus.

PHILOCTETES

They hurt *you*? A wrong that maddened you?

NEOPTOLEMUS

Oh, I wish I could act on my resentment,
then both Mycenae and Sparta would learn
that Scyros has also given great sons birth.

PHILOCTETES

Well said, my son, but I must understand   260
about your anger: why, what charge, why you're here?

NEOPTOLEMUS

That's not easy for me, I'll try to explain
what I suffered at their hands.
When Fate determined Achilles' death . . .

PHILOCTETES

What? Enough . . . But he's dead?

NEOPTOLEMUS
Dead. Killed by Phoebus, not by a man, pierced
by an arrow from the bow of god.

PHILOCTETES
High lineage in killer and victim, what
to do first, open your griefs or weep for him?

NEOPTOLEMUS
You have enough pain, dear Philoctetes,   270
without crying for me.

PHILOCTETES
That's true. So tell me again, from the start,
how they hurt *you.*

NEOPTOLEMUS
Odysseus and my father's foster-father, Phoenix,
sent for me in a bright ship, told me,
true or not, my dead father's power
had descended to me, that only *my* hand
would topple Troy. I yielded and sailed.
How I lusted to see my father in his death,
My father I'd never seen alive, and I was flattered: 280
without me Troy was lost to us.
On the second day swift by sail and oar
we'd reached Sigeum. I hate that name.
Those men all honored me: "you're Achilles come back to us."
There lay my father dead, and me, poor fool, I mourned him
a while and accepted the Atridae almost as family,
claimed my father's arms, and, inconceivable, they said:
"Child of Achilles, whatever was your father's yours.
But not his arms, assigned to Laertes' son."
I cried out, I got up furious, and I spoke bitterly   290
to Odysseus: "You, how dare you give these arms
to any man but me? They're mine by right.

I've given *you* no right." Then Odysseus said:
"Yes, boy, I have the right. I rescued
the body and arms of your father Achilles." That
maddened me, I burned with abuse and insult, none
adequate for that gross embezzler, who said, stung but so calm:
"You weren't with us, you managed to stay away.
Try this response to your boasting and your arrogance:
You'll never reach Scyros with these arms."   300
In the sleet of attacks like those I left.
And now I'm sailing home, the victim of Odysseus the Burglar.
And yet he's less to blame than rulers.
Each soldier is subject to authority,
all crimes spring from the seed of poor teachings.
That's my story. Whoever hates the Atridae
will find me his friend, as I hope he'll find the gods.

CHORUS
O mother Earth,
mother of Zeus,
ultimate provider, the golden   310
Pactolus river courses
between its golden shores
through your body. You were riding
your team of lions, and I called to you
when the Atridae dishonored themselves
that day, diverted from Neoptolemus
the arms of his father, shining Achilles,
to hand over to Odysseus, Laertes' son.

PHILOCTETES
You good men bring me a token of shared pain.
I can just see Odysseus' hand and tongue   320
at their conspiratorial work, anything as long as false.
No surprise there. But did Ajax see and bear all this?

NEOPTOLEMUS
My friend, Ajax was dead. Otherwise
my rights would have been respected.

PHILOCTETES
    Oh, is he dead, too?

NEOPTOLEMUS
    Yes. He's left the light.

PHILOCTETES
    Yes. *He* has. But not those who should never have seen it.

NEOPTOLEMUS
    Those prevail, and the Argives call them "mighty."

PHILOCTETES
    And my old good friend Nestor, is he
    alive? His wisdom often checked their intemperateness.   330

NEOPTOLEMUS
    He's not what he was since he lost
    his most loved son Antilochus.

PHILOCTETES
    Oh, the two men I could spare the least.
    Your account inflicts a double loss.
    Oh, what hope when two men like that die and Odysseus
    survives, Odysseus—why not *him*? Why?

NEOPTOLEMUS
    A crafty gamesman, but you know
    they're the ones who commonly lose.

PHILOCTETES
    Tell me, where was Patroclus, once
    your father's dearest friend?   340

NEOPTOLEMUS
    Dead like the rest. It's true: war
    spares the villain and dooms the decent man.

PHILOCTETES

My life tells me that too: and about another,
worthless, shrewd and glib.

NEOPTOLEMUS

Odysseus?

PHILOCTETES

No. Thersites, who babbled when silence
mattered. Does he live?

NEOPTOLEMUS

I didn't see him, but heard he lives.

PHILOCTETES

I thought so. Evil never dies. Are the gods
perverse? I think they turn back hopelessly bad men   350
from the mouth of hell but trample the righteous.
Or, if the gods are unjust, how to find them just?

NEOPTOLEMUS

I will avoid the men who irrigate villainy.
I will see the Atridae and Troy only from a great distance.
I will sail to my native rocks in Scyros island; they
will do for me. Love and farewell, Philoctetes.
May the gods hear your heart's cry and heal you.
We go now and ready the ship for the moment
when the gods grant us a favorable wind.

PHILOCTETES

You leave so soon, my son?   360

NEOPTOLEMUS

It's time to go and watch the tide from the beach.

PHILOCTETES
    Oh, in your father's and mother's name, by all
    the household gods, my son, don't leave me here alone,
    I beg you, abandoned to the pains you've seen
    and worse ones you've been told about. Think of me
    as a stowaway. I know it's burdensome.
    Please take on the burden—the high spirit weighs shame and
           honor.
    It would dirty your honor to leave me here. Fame
    and glory are yours if you bear me alive to Oeta.
    Please. It's just a day's bother. Take heart. Stow me   370
    wherever you like, the hold, the bow, the stem, whatever,
    wherever I'm least likely to offend.
    By Zeus, the god of suppliants, please take me. Look, I'm falling
    at your feet, me the cripple. Don't condemn me
    to this empty place. Take me safe to your home.
    Or take me to Euboea. From there I can cross to Oeta
    to the Trachinian passes, to the broad Spercheus river
    to see my father once more, these heavy years
    filled with nightmares of his possible death . . . Every time
    visitors came I sent word to him, would he   380
    fetch me home in his own ship. He's dead, I suppose.
    Or the bearers of my message dismissed me
    from their cares and hurried home. But you, now,
    my messenger and my savior, please, pity me.
    You understand how fortune and misfortune stand
    on slippery ground. So the prospering man at ease
    should look for the rocks ahead.
    The unexpected shipwreck waits.

CHORUS
    Prince,
    pity   390
    this agony of grief.
    May the gods keep any friend of mine
    from such an end.

Pity.
I know the pungent bitterness
of your hate for the Atridae. Turn their rotten plot
to this poor man's profit.
Take him home.
Bear him through the waves on our ship,
away from the Avengers.   400

NEOPTOLEMUS
You must hold to your compassion.
If it's only a passing mood, the closeness of his wound
may shake and wither it.

CHORUS
I'll be true.

NEOPTOLEMUS
I couldn't bear the shame
of not helping a stranger in pain.
I couldn't lag behind
the light of your insistence, so
we'll sail. Let him board. I cannot think
our ship will reject him. May the gods   410
bring us home safe and soon.

PHILOCTETES
The day now glows. I'm happy.
How can I prove my heart's thanks to you,
my dearest friend, and to you kind sailors?
My son, we leave, but, before we leave, go in
and recognize this homeless home, enter into
my heavy life and the obstinacy of my hanging on.
I think no other man could have lasted.
But I learned from the needs that were my Fate.
(Neoptolemus and Philoctetes start to enter the cave.)

CHORUS
   Wait. Two men are coming, one a sailor,   420
   one a stranger. Let's see what they want first.
(Two sailors enter; one, disguised as a merchant captain, speaks.)

SAILOR
   Son of Achilles, I'm docked next to you by accident.
   I asked this shipmate of yours, on guard with two others,
   where you were. I command a ship that's sailing home
   from Ilium to Peparethus, rich in wines.
   I found the crew on liberty was yours
   and decided, as a man should, to tell you
   what you probably don't suspect:
   the Argives' plans against you, I mean their plots.

NEOPTOLEMUS
   I won't forget your concern. Say more clearly   430
   what the Greeks will do to me.

SAILOR
   Old Phoenix and the sons of Theseus
   are after you in a warship.

NEOPTOLEMUS
   To bring me back, or to force me back?

SAILOR
   I don't know; that's all I heard.

NEOPTOLEMUS
   Is it to please the Atridae that Phoenix and his cohorts . . . ?

SAILOR
   I can't say; they're coming.

NEOPTOLEMUS
   And why didn't Odysseus come himself—afraid?

SAILOR
　　He and Tydeus' son were searching for someone else.

NEOPTOLEMUS
　　Who? For whom would Odysseus sail on his own?   440

SAILOR
　　He . . . wait; who's this next to you? Whisper.

NEOPTOLEMUS
　　This is world-famous Philoctetes.

SAILOR
　　No more talking. Go. Get away from here immediately.

PHILOCTETES
　　Boy, what's he saying, and why in whispers,
　　as if I were a thing?

NEOPTOLEMUS *(sotto voce)*
　　I don't know yet. But he'll tell us all. Out loud.

SAILOR
　　Give secrets away, child of Achilles? I'm poor
　　and owe the commanders some regard. They've paid me well.

NEOPTOLEMUS
　　They're my enemies. Philoctetes here, because he hates them,
　　is now my dearest friend. If you come   450
　　"as a man should," to help, you must say what you know.

SAILOR
　　You don't realize what you're asking.

NEOPTOLEMUS
　　I do.

SAILOR
The consequences . . .

NEOPTOLEMUS
are mine.

SAILOR
Well, Odysseus and Tydeus' son are headed here
to take this man, by persuasion or force.
They've sworn an oath to do it. Bold Odysseus proclaimed
his purpose in public, his reputation's now at stake.

NEOPTOLEMUS
Why now? All these years. They'd left this man   460
and forgotten him. Is it compassion? Is it the fear
of retribution, the anger of the gods?

SAILOR
I'll tell you some things you don't know.
I'll tell you about a prophet of high lineage,
Helenus son of Priam, seized by foxy Odysseus
in a night's prowl. Who else but rotten Odysseus
would tie him up and show him off to the Argives?
Helenus said, "You'll never take Troy
unless you get Philoctetes from Lemnos to help you."
Odysseus took on the job. He would bring the man,   470
willing or not. "If I fail," he said, "anyone here
can have my head." That's it. Beware, you and your friend.

PHILOCTETES
That sneak and burglar really swore to take me
back to those Greeks? That's as likely as death
loosing me because some one has said a prayer.

SAILOR
I can't say. Back to my ship now. So goodbye.
The gods be with you both and order all things well.
(*Exit sailors.*)

PHILOCTETES
>I can't believe it, boy, that Odysseus
>would seduce me to his ship, exhibit me to those Greeks.
>Monstrous. I'd rather deal with the snake   480
>that crippled me. Nothing's too low
>for Odysseus. He'll come. Hurry, my boy, let's put
>the ocean between him and us. Now's the time
>to work, when we rest we'll rest peacefully.

NEOPTOLEMUS
>The wind's in our teeth. When it drops.

PHILOCTETES
>All winds favor the man who's running from evil.

NEOPTOLEMUS
>Not this wind, even for him.

PHILOCTETES
>For pirates looking to rob and pillage
>any wind will do.

NEOPTOLEMUS
>All right. We'll sail. Take what you want from the cave.   490

PHILOCTETES
>I haven't got much, but need a little.

NEOPTOLEMUS
>My ship has what you'll need.

PHILOCTETES
>Not that wonderful herb that quiets my pain.

NEOPTOLEMUS
>Bring it with you. What else?

PHILOCTETES
  I may by chance have dropped some arrows
  anyone could pick up. Let me go look.
  (Philoctetes goes into his cave, returns with bow and arrows.)

NEOPTOLEMUS
  What you're holding, is that the famous bow?

PHILOCTETES
  It is.

NEOPTOLEMUS
  Let me get closer to it. May I handle it,
  worship it like a god?   500

PHILOCTETES
  That and whatever else I can do to please you.

NEOPTOLEMUS
  It's true my longing masters me.
  If it seems improper, I'll withdraw.

PHILOCTETES
  Thank you for that. But you have the right
  to this privilege. You alone
  give me daylight,
  and Oeta,
  and my old father,
  and my friends. I was the lowest of the low
  and you uplifted me above the heads   510
  of my tormentors. The bow is yours
  to handle and return. Think of it: your service
  makes you the only man to have earned *that*.
  The bow came to *me* for kindling
  the funeral pyre of Heracles.

NEOPTOLEMUS
I've found a friend, and hope I am one.
Some men recognize good done to them
and give of themselves in turn. They know
a friend outweighs, outshines, mocks an infinity of gold.
Go on inside now.   520

PHILOCTETES
I will. Please come too. My wound needs you.
(They go into the cave.)

CHORUS
Not from out of my own life but from the tradition,
a story that turns out to be true: of a youth
who dared to approach Zeus' bed.
Cronus' great son
bound him for endless torture
to the endless round of the wheel.
Aside from him,
what life known or heard of is sadder
than Philoctetes'? Innocent man,   530
dragging to his end,
he robbed or wronged no man.
How can I understand him? I see
the waves of the years of his anguish
break and break on the gray cold stone.
He is his own neighbor, he groans
to his neighbor, limping through the heavy
round of day on day on day,
no friend to mirror his misery to him, to offer
healing attentiveness, to calm the rage   540
and quell the pain
with herbs from the good soil.
No choice: between spasms his infant's crawling's
all he can manage on his hunt for his drugs.
Alone among the sons of men he's cast out of earth's

gifts, the sowing and the reaping.
Enough if now and then his arrow downs
any living thing. Poor man,
in those ten black years
what did he find to drink—   550
not wine but stagnant water?

He's found a good friend now.
The music of his life deepens
through his suffering; he will rediscover a green
continuity.
Goodbye to the black months.
Homing in with our ship
to his Spercheus' banks, his old
countryside, the Naiads' woods, he will roam,
where the hero of the brazen shield   560
climbed in fire to the sky over Oeta.
(Neoptolemus and Philoctetes reappear from within the cave.)

NEOPTOLEMUS
    Go on in if you feel like it. Why
    so quiet all of a sudden?

PHILOCTETES
    Oh, no.

NEOPTOLEMUS
    What?

PHILOCTETES
    Nothing, boy. Go on.

NEOPTOLEMUS
    You feel the pain again?

PHILOCTETES
    No, just a tiny . . . I think it's going away—O god!

NEOPTOLEMUS
   What is it—groaning like that, calling on god?

PHILOCTETES
   To help me, to rescue me, oh . . .   570

NEOPTOLEMUS
   Please, what's wrong? Won't you tell me? You won't
   talk to me? I'm not blind or deaf. What is it?

PHILOCTETES
   My son, I'm lost. I can't
   hide it from you any more. Lost. It shoots through me,
   shoots through me, can't, oh it hurts so much, utterly
   wasted, O my son, eating me up, my son. Ogod/ogod,
   ogod/ogod/ogod/ogod/ogod/ogod/ogod/ogod/ogod/ogod,
   a sword my son, if you have a sword at hand, cut
   my foot off. Whatever else, my life, forget it. Quick,
   quick my son, quickly.   580

NEOPTOLEMUS
   What is it all of a sudden? You're crying.

PHILOCTETES
   You know.

NEOPTOLEMUS
   What is it?

PHILOCTETES
   You know.

NEOPTOLEMUS
   No. What's the matter?

PHILOCTETES
   Don't you know? Ogod/ogod/ogod.

NEOPTOLEMUS
Oh, Philoctetes, you're in such pain again.

PHILOCTETES
Beyond words. Oh, pity me.

NEOPTOLEMUS
What shall I do?

PHILOCTETES
Don't be afraid of me. Stay with me. My pain   590
lets me be, then comes back home after its holiday.

NEOPTOLEMUS
Poor man, all this misery, lean on me, let me help you.

PHILOCTETES
No, please don't touch me. Take my bow, you wanted to hold it.
Take it, care for it until my shaking stops and sleep comes.
That's medicine, follows the drowsiness after the spasm.
So let me sleep then, and if they come,
keep it. It can't be theirs.
It can't be theirs, however you hold on to it, force,
Foxiness. Do it or you're twice a murderer:
death for you and for me your suppliant.   600

NEOPTOLEMUS
It's yours and mine alone, I swear it, I swear
I'll do what's needed. Let me have the bow
and good luck attend it.

PHILOCTETES
Take it my son, but first propitiate
the Jealous God. This bow: for its first owner
a plague, and for me; don't let it be for you.
(*Philoctetes hands the bow to Neoptolemus.*)

NEOPTOLEMUS
  May the gods look on us kindly; whatever way
  we're destined to go, may the trip prosper.

PHILOCTETES
  O my son, your prayers may be useless. Look
  at my wound, the flow of this black blood's a sign   610
  of worse to come. Oh, how I hate this foot, now
  pain, later increase of pain. It prowls and stalks,
  I know it will spring on me. Oh, now that you know,
  please stay with me, stay with me.
  If only I could rivet this spasm forever in Odysseus' chest . . .
  And those two generals—Menelaus, Agamemnon—may the
            worm
  reign in their guts as long as it has in mine.
  And you, Death, I call on you every day. Death, you
  don't answer me. My boy, noble boy, take me, burn me
  in those fires. Consume me. I did such a service   620
  for Heracles, Zeus' son, and received the bow you're holding.
  Answer me. Why don't you talk to me?

NEOPTOLEMUS
  I was thinking about your endless pain, my heart
  so heavy.

PHILOCTETES
  Understand, this pain leaves as it comes, fast,
  but don't leave me here by myself.

NEOPTOLEMUS
  Courage. We'll stay.

PHILOCTETES
  You will?

NEOPTOLEMUS
  I promise.

PHILOCTETES
>It wouldn't be right to swear you to that.   630

NEOPTOLEMUS
>My honor's at stake: I couldn't leave you.

PHILOCTETES
>Give me your hand on it.

NEOPTOLEMUS
>Here. My pledge.

PHILOCTETES
>Over there then, I'll go . . .

NEOPTOLEMUS
>Where?

PHILOCTETES
>Up.

NEOPTOLEMUS
>Are you delirious again? Why
>are you staring up at the sky?

PHILOCTETES
>Let me go, let me go.

NEOPTOLEMUS
>Let you go where?   640

PHILOCTETES
>I tell you, let me go.

NEOPTOLEMUS
>No.

PHILOCTETES
  Don't touch me or I'll die.

NEOPTOLEMUS
  I'm letting you go. You're calmer now.

PHILOCTETES
  O mother Earth, take me in my last sickness.
  I'm dying now and can't even stand on you.
  (Philoctetes falls.)

NEOPTOLEMUS
  I think he'll be asleep soon: his head's falling
  back, sweat trickles over his body, a black
  and bloody mess breaks out of his foot. Friends,
  let's leave him in peace till he falls asleep.   650

CHORUS
  Lord Sleep, breathe
  a quiet music for him.
  Lord of peace not pain,
  flow in your calm over his eyes. Come
  lord healer, come.

  Boy, consider where you are and how
  you might go. Consider
  and be clear. Why wait? This time
  right now is the ready fruit.

NEOPTOLEMUS
  We could sail on alone, we could   660
  steal the bow, we could not succeed
  without him. The god said so. This man
  crowns our victory. Otherwise we're shameful frauds.

CHORUS

    Boy, leave the burden of such thoughts
    with the god and whisper
    your answer in my ear.
    The sick man sleeps lightly, he can hear
    in his febrility, his closed eyes see.

    Boy, if your plan still holds,
    work it out privately now. Do I need   670
    to repeat it? There's no doubt his endless torments
    stretch vastly ahead.
    It's a fair wind boy, and there he lies,
    gladly asleep in the sun, deaf and blind,
    his feet and his hands like those of Earth's buried guests,
    absolutely still.
    May this whole scene be your teacher,
    and let me say shortest way round is best.

NEOPTOLEMUS

    Quiet, and be alert. His eyes
    are opening, his head's moving.   680

PHILOCTETES

    How wonderful, waking to brightness with you
    near me, concerned about me.
    I never hoped for that, never dared.
    The Atridae, those courageous captains,
    had no heart to accept my cries
    and my wound. I afflicted their eyes, I insulted their ears, my
                    hurt
    was foul in their nostrils. But you have a noble nature, my son,
    and made light of all that.
    A space of peace seems to have come.
    Absence of pain.   690
    So help me up, my boy, up onto my feet.
    Soon, the attack spent, we'll sail.

NEOPTOLEMUS

How glad I am to see you, so happy
and amazed you're well and free of pain.
To look at you before was almost
to look at death.
Can you get up now? Or should these men lift you?
They won't mind in the least since you and I
Have come to an understanding.

PHILOCTETES

Thank you, my son, but would you do it?   700
If they carry me I may sicken them.
My wound. The smell of my wound.
Not yet for that closeness. Soon they'll be my shipmates,
and I think that voyage will ask of them
all that they have to give.

NEOPTOLEMUS *(sotto voce)*

Very well. Get up now. Hold on to me.

PHILOCTETES

Don't be afraid. I'm used to this.

NEOPTOLEMUS

O, my God, what do I do now?

PHILOCTETES

What's wrong? Your words are drifting strangely.

NEOPTOLEMUS

I don't know what to say. I'm at a loss.   710

PHILOCTETES

But why? Don't say that, my son.

NEOPTOLEMUS

It's true. I have no choice.

PHILOCTETES

    Are you disgusted at my wound?
    Is that stopping you now from taking me?

NEOPTOLEMUS

    Everything's disgusting when a man denies
    his essential self, his acts violating his understanding.

PHILOCTETES

    Look, you're helping me. Nothing in all of this
    can sully your lineage.

NEOPTOLEMUS

    Time will uncover my treachery; that tortures me.

PHILOCTETES

    Not in what you're doing now; but your words . . .   720

NEOPTOLEMUS

    O Zeus, what shall I do? To be shown up twice—
    hide what I shouldn't and persist in the lie . . .

PHILOCTETES

    Unless I'm wrong, this man will betray me
    and will leave me stranded here.

NEOPTOLEMUS

    Leave you? No not that. Far worse: bring you
    with us. That's what tortures me.

PHILOCTETES

    Strange words, their meanings hidden from me.

NEOPTOLEMUS

    Well, here it is, straight out. You're sailing
    for Troy, to the Atridae, to all those Greeks.

PHILOCTETES
Oh, no!   730

NEOPTOLEMUS
Can you listen to me quietly?

PHILOCTETES
"Listen to me," he says, and what now for me?

NEOPTOLEMUS
Well, first to rescue you from this terror,
then waste Troy—with your help.

PHILOCTETES
Would you do that, really do that?

NEOPTOLEMUS
There's no choice. Try to accept it.

PHILOCTETES
You, how rotten you are, so hard to believe this betrayal.
Give me the bow, I want the bow, give me back my bow, now.

NEOPTOLEMUS
Impossible. I owe my chiefs allegiance
and share their sense of necessity.   740

PHILOCTETES
And can you look me in the face, fire,
monster, you've really done me in, haven't you?
Champ, champion, oh how I hate you, master
of treachery. And me the suppliant, me
you rob of my bow, my life.
Oh, give it back, I beg of you, my son.
If you feel for me at all, give it back.

Don't take my life away.
Oh, he turns away, says nothing, meaning
he'll never part with it.   750
I'm crying out to you rivers, headlands, lairs
of wild beasts, sharp cliffs, only you—
lasting witnesses of my pain—will listen to me.
Listen to the torment brought to me
by Achilles' son:
He swore to bring me home; it's Troy I go to.
Our hands sealed a contract, and he borrowed the bow.
Now it's his, the sacred bow of Zeus' son Heracles.
And he'll flaunt it in front of the Argives,
and me as well, as if he'd taken a strong man,   760
and doesn't understand he's killing the dead,
a shadow, a diaphanous ghost.
He could never take a healthy Philoctetes.
And even as I am, a cripple, he still needed guile.
I'm trapped now. Oh, what can I do?
Please give my bow back to me,
be your true self again. Will you?
No answer. Lost.
Cave with a double entrance. I'm back
to you once more, but without arms and so   770
without food. I'll wither and die here. The quarry
of bird and beast I pursued will now pursue me,
those who served as food will feed on the hunter,
blood for blood. This man's innocent posture
earns me my death.

I curse your life—no I'll wait
until I know if you'll go the other way.
If not, may my curse wither you.

CHORUS

What shall we do? It's up to you, prince.
Do we sail, or do what he asks?   780

NEOPTOLEMUS

>I feel a strange pity. From the very start
>I've been moved with pity for this man.

PHILOCTETES

>Please be merciful. Do you want to be known
>as the shrewd liar who betrayed me?

NEOPTOLEMUS

>What shall I do? I wish I'd never left Scyros
>to experience this awful circumstance.

PHILOCTETES

>You're not a bad man, but learned your foul part
>from evil people. Leave that for those
>naturally corrupt. Sail, but first return my bow.

NEOPTOLEMUS

>Well, men. What shall we do?   790
>(*Odysseus appears suddenly.*)

ODYSSEUS

>Are you crazy? Give me that bow.

PHILOCTETES

>Who's that? Is that Odysseus' voice?

ODYSSEUS

>As you see. Odysseus. Me.

PHILOCTETES

>Now I'm really sold out. It was Odysseus
>who captured me and stole my bow.

ODYSSEUS

>Yes. I. I did it.

PHILOCTETES
Son, give me back my bow.

ODYSSEUS
That he won't, even if he wants to. In fact,
either you come along with it or we'll drag you with us.

PHILOCTETES
You corrupt, arrogant . . . These people   800
of yours will take me by force?

ODYSSEUS
Yes, if you don't come freely.

PHILOCTETES
O Lemnos, you with your volcanic fires
lit through Hephaestus' fall, will you
allow this man to rip me away from you?

ODYSSEUS
It's Zeus, Zeus who rules here, Zeus
who gives the orders; I do his will.

PHILOCTETES
How disgusting—to invoke the gods
and put lies in their months.

ODYSSEUS
It's the truth. You must come,   810
you must travel the appointed road.

PHILOCTETES
I will not.

ODYSSEUS
I say yes. You must.

PHILOCTETES
  I must have been born to pain.
  Did my father give birth to a slave?

ODYSSEUS
  No, to one among equals of high lineage
  with whom you will destroy Troy.

PHILOCTETES
  Never. Anything but that as long as this sharp
  precipice thrusts its harshness under me.

ODYSSEUS
  What would you do?   820

PHILOCTETES
  Throw myself down and shatter
  my head in the rocks underneath.

ODYSSEUS *(to Chorus)*
  Hold him, both his arms, tight.
  (The Chorus members grasp Philoctetes.)

PHILOCTETES
  O my hands, how weak you are, imprisoned
  by that man, all because my bow's gone.
  You've done it again, haven't you, con man,
  fungus heart rot, using this stranger, just a boy,
  to get at me. He grieves right now
  for his rashness and the wrong done to me.
  In fact, he's too good for you and stands   830
  appropriately alongside me. But you, like a shadow
  voice you were always
  giving the boy his cues,
  and he studied at your vicious school
  against his own characteristic grain.
  And now, you sickening cheat, you intend to wrap me

in rope and carry me from this island where
you first left me homeless and alone, living dead.
My curse on your life. I've spent
so many years cursing you. But the gods   840
embitter my life, and you dance on
as my endless misery defines my life.
You laugh at me, you and Atreus' two sons
who mock me as well; you tried
to escape induction by playing mad.
But they put your son in front of your plow
and they had you, forced you to sail with them.
Though I volunteered my seven ships and me,
I was marooned, they say by you and you by them.
So I'm dead to you, why seize the corpse?   850
The gods despise you.
I still limp, my wound still stinks. I'll still sour
your rites and sacrifices. My curse on your life
for what you've done to me. If the gods are just
you will be cursed. I know they're just
because they touched your hearts to think of me
and come here. O my own country,
and you watchful gods, avenge me, however
long it takes, if you pity me as I deserve.
If I could see them shattered I'd be almost free of pain.   860

CHORUS

He's full of spite, and hard. Suffering
hasn't gentled him.

ODYSSEUS

I haven't time to say more than this;
I'm a man who fits the occasion.
When it requires even-handedness, justice, that's
what I furnish. I always want to win
except in your case. I give in freely.
You sailors let him go. He can stay.

We don't need you, Philoctetes, we have
your bow, we have two great bowmen, Teucer   870
and myself, who can shoot with your skill.
Who needs you? You can keep
your Lemnos. We go. Your prize
may earn for me the honor you'd have had.

PHILOCTETES
What can I do? And you strutting
for the Greeks in my arms . . .

ODYSSEUS
Enough talk. I'm leaving.

PHILOCTETES *(to Neoptolemus)*
Son of Achilles, are you going, too?
Not a word from you?

ODYSSEUS
Let's go, Neoptolemus, and don't look at him.   880
You'll spoil everything.

PHILOCTETES *(to Chorus)*
And you men, you'll leave me by myself now?
No pity in you?

CHORUS
This young man, our captain, governs
what we say. He's our law.

NEOPTOLEMUS
I know Odysseus will call me weak.
But if Philoctetes wants you men to stay with him
until we finish our prayers and our preparations,
do so. Maybe he'll relent. So we go.
When we call you, come on the double   890
(Odysseus and Neoptolemus leave.)

PHILOCTETES
    Cave in the rock, I'm married to you forever.
    Hot and freezing by turns, you'll witness my death.
    Tell me, sad home, haunted by my suffering,
    how will I go on?
    I free all the birds, their flight now
    endless, wherever they land they've won
    immunity from me and my bow.

CHORUS
    It's you, you've fashioned your own doom.
    Don't blame the gods for your stubbornness.
    Faced with the good you chose otherwise.   900

PHILOCTETES
    O endless, endless unhappiness,
    totally wasted by unhappiness,
    barely lingering, hanging on
    without a single friend
    to accompany me to my end.
    My arrows' work on Lemnos done forever,
    the hunting season of my life is dead.
    I suspected nothing and the liar seduced me.
    I'd love to see him fixed in my agony.

CHORUS
    Fate, fate, not the works of our hands,   910
    threw you down. Don't curse us, we cared
    for you and we care for you now.

PHILOCTETES
    Odysseus sits on the sand by the gray sea
    and laughs at Philoctetes.
    He plays with my bow; it was my life.

    O my bow, how I loved you,
    mine the only hands that bent you.

If you could feel, what power of grief.
They've forced us apart, you from me, Heracles' friend.
A bad man is stringing you, you serve a master   920
of deceit—shareholder in that company of men
who have hurt me.

CHORUS

A man should stand his righteous ground
but moderate his venom's toxin.
As for Odysseus, he represents the communal will,
which he obeys, which speaks through him.

PHILOCTETES

You birds, once my bright-eyed prey
in these hills, keep flying near the hunter's home.
Untouchable, you own the air.
My hands hang, the bow's gone and with it your caution.   930
Your weakened enemy's flesh will turn
into your food. Come, do your will
as I diminish into starvation, the only
voyage left.

CHORUS

Can you still open yourself to a friend? If so, listen.
It's you who feed your pain and grief.
You can choose your freedom.

PHILOCTETES

Of all the men who've come to Lemnos,
you've touched my heart, but also rekindled
the old grief. Why afflict the afflicted?   940

CHORUS

What do you mean?

PHILOCTETES

I mean, you want to take me to hateful Troy.

CHORUS
For your sake too.

PHILOCTETES
Then go. Now.
(Chorus starts to leave.)

CHORUS
Good. Good. We will. Men, to the ship and our oars.

PHILOCTETES
Please, please in God's name stay.

CHORUS *(coming back)*
Calm yourself.

PHILOCTETES
Please. Stay.

CHORUS
Why?

PHILOCTETES
O dark darkest spirit, it's over for me. 950
Damn foot, what will I do with it?
Friends, please come back.

CHORUS
What do you want? You say
"Go." You say "Come back."

PHILOCTETES
Don't be angry. Man in pain
undergoes the rash cries of his own discord.

CHORUS
Unhappy man, come sail with us.

PHILOCTETES
>   Never, never. If the God of the Lightning
>   fixed me with his lance of fire,
>   I'd still say "never."   960
>   Let Ilium die and all those in the siege
>   whose hardened hearts were pleased
>   to throw me out and let me rot.
>   May I make just one request?

CHORUS
>   What?

PHILOCTETES
>   Let me have a sword, an axe, whatever.

CHORUS
>   Why? To do what?

PHILOCTETES
>   To shred my body, to rid it of its limbs.
>   Blood, blood suffuses my thoughts.

CHORUS
>   But why?   970

PHILOCTETES
>   I want to find my father.

CHORUS
>   Where?

PHILOCTETES
>   Down in death's house.
>   He's gone from earth. Oh, how much
>   I long for my city where I was born,

the sacred stream encircling my house. I left
to help the Greeks who have destroyed me.
(Philoctetes goes into his cave.)

CHORUS
    I should have gone to the ship by now,
    but I saw Odysseus coming near
    with Neoptolemus.   980
(Odysseus and Neoptolemus, with the bow, reenter, talking with each
other.)

ODYSSEUS
    Why are you going back so fast?

NEOPTOLEMUS
    To undo what I've committed.

ODYSSEUS
    What does that mean?

NEOPTOLEMUS
    I shouldn't have obeyed the Greeks and you.

ODYSSEUS
    What did you do that was so terrible?

NEOPTOLEMUS
    I lied. I betrayed a man.

ODYSSEUS
    Who? I hope you're not verging on something rash.

NEOPTOLEMUS
    No, nothing rash. I've got to see the son of Poeas.

ODYSSEUS
    Why? Your words are upsetting me.

NEOPTOLEMUS
I'm going to return the bow.   990

ODYSSEUS
O Zeus—give it back, you can't mean that!

NEOPTOLEMUS
I'm ashamed of how I got it.

ODYSSEUS
You can't be serious.

NEOPTOLEMUS
I am, unless you think seriousness is a joke.

ODYSSEUS
Achilles' son, exactly what are you saying?

NEOPTOLEMUS
Do I have to repeat myself?

ODYSSEUS
I wish I hadn't heard you in the first place.

NEOPTOLEMUS
I have nothing else to say.

ODYSSEUS
There's someone who'll stop you.

NEOPTOLEMUS
Who?   1000

ODYSSEUS
The whole Greek army, me among them.

NEOPTOLEMUS
> You're a shrewd man, Odysseus,
> but your words are foolish.

ODYSSEUS
> And you're foolish not only in words
> but in your acts as well.

NEOPTOLEMUS
> Better just than clever.

ODYSSEUS
> Is that justice—to give back
> what I helped you get?

NEOPTOLEMUS
> I lied. I'm ashamed of that.
> I want to make amends.   1010

ODYSSEUS
> And the Greeks. You're not afraid of their response?

NEOPTOLEMUS
> I'm more afraid of being unjust.

ODYSSEUS
> Your justice will face our power.

NEOPTOLEMUS
> You can't make me do what I won't.

ODYSSEUS
> Then we'll fight *you*, not the Trojans.

NEOPTOLEMUS
> Whatever comes, comes.

ODYSSEUS
You see my hand near my sword?

NEOPTOLEMUS
Be ready for me to do as much, quickly.

ODYSSEUS
I'm going, and I will tell the army.
They'll punish you.   1020

NEOPTOLEMUS
Very cautious of you. Such discretion
may keep you alive indefinitely.
(Exit Odysseus.)
Philoctetes, son of Poeas, come out of your cave.

PHILOCTETES *(from within the cave)*
What's this noise at my door?
What do you want with me?
(appears at the cave's mouth)
I don't like what I see. Some new terror
to top the old ones?

NEOPTOLEMUS
Wait a minute. I have news.

PHILOCTETES
I'm afraid. Last time you came
I believed you and suffered for it.   1030

NEOPTOLEMUS
Can a man be sorry?

PHILOCTETES
You sounded sweet as this in your treachery
when you stole my bow.

NEOPTOLEMUS
> I'm not lying to you. I want to know
> if you're completely sure about staying.

PHILOCTETES
> You can stop right now.

NEOPTOLEMUS
> You have no doubts?

PHILOCTETES
> Absolutely none.

NEOPTOLEMUS
> If I could have convinced you to come,
> I would. But there's no point. So I'll stop.   1040

PHILOCTETES
> You might as well stop talking. Did you really think
> we could ever be friends again? You lied, stole
> my life, and came preaching, rotten son
> of a great father. Damn you all, the Atridae,
> Odysseus, and you.

NEOPTOLEMUS
> You can stop cursing now. Here's your bow.

PHILOCTETES
> What? Another trick?

NEOPTOLEMUS
> No. I swear by Olympian Zeus.

PHILOCTETES
> If these words are true, they're wonderful.

NEOPTOLEMUS
>Believe me. Stretch out your hand. Here's your bow.   1050
(Odysseus appears as Neoptolemus gives Philoctetes his bow.)

ODYSSEUS
>Stop. As the gods witness, and in the name
>of the Atridae and all the Greeks.

PHILOCTETES
>Whose voice my son? Was that Odysseus?

ODYSSEUS
>Yes it is, here to carry you to Troy.
>I don't care what Neoptolemus thinks.

PHILOCTETES
>If this arrow flies straight,
>You'll regret your words.

NEOPTOLEMUS
>Stop! in the gods' name don't shoot.

PHILOCTETES
>By the gods, dear boy, let my hands go.

NEOPTOLEMUS
>I won't.   1060

PHILOCTETES
>Why did you stop me
>from killing the man I hate?

NEOPTOLEMUS
>Would you be proud of that? Would I?
(Odysseus leaves quickly.)

PHILOCTETES

    One thing's clear. The generals, the Greeks'
    lying heralds, talk big, and run fast.

NEOPTOLEMUS

    Whatever. The bow's yours again. You have
    no further quarrel with me.

PHILOCTETES

    None, my boy. You've shown what you're made of,
    sprung not from Sisyphus but Achilles, noblest
    in life as now in death.   1070

NEOPTOLEMUS

    What you say about my father and me
    makes me happy. But now, a request.
    A man must bear the fate the gods dictate.
    But some, like you, are attached to their wounds.
    Who can pity or accept such self-destruction?
    You listen to no one, a friend who loves you,
    who tries to talk to you, becomes your enemy.
    Nevertheless as Zeus is my witness I'll say
    what I have to. Inscribe
    these words in your mind forever: 1080
    Your wound results from the anger of the god,
    that you blundered into Chryse's roofless
    sacred place and stirred the serpent guardian.
    There's no relief for you in the endless rerun
    of the sun's courses,
    until you come to Troy freely.
    There our healing Asclepiadae will ready you
    to stand with your bow and me, to conquer Troy.
    I'll tell you how I know this: it's from
    our Trojan prisoner, the prophet Helenus.   1090
    He also said that Troy must crack
    this summer, his life on it.

Now that you know, come, please,
willingly. Look at your future—healed, hailed
as preeminent in war and prince
who closed the agonized chapter of Troy.

PHILOCTETES

Oh, how I hate this life that reins me in
from the darkness, I long
to gallop into the grave, and, my friend,
what will I do, my dear friend who tells me go back,   1100
back to those I can barely look at, who'll have to say
welcome to me, and will have to forgive me?
What my eyes have already seen has almost closed them,
and soon they must see me eating and sleeping
with Atreus' sons, my murderers,
with Odysseus, the well-head of my misery . . .

I could forget the long flow of my pain.
But what about tomorrow? Don't I know by now
about all those infected minds waiting
to drown me in their pus? And what about you, you   1110
should talk me into staying here, and stay away from Troy.
They've defrauded you, stolen your father's arms,
and you want to help them fight, and send me too?
No. You promised to take me home. Do it.
You go to Scyros and let those vipers rot
from each other's fluid poisons. Your father and I
will thank you. If you help the killer, you become him.

NEOPTOLEMUS

What you say makes sense. Still,
I wish you'd believe the god's promises
and mine. I'm your friend. Trust me. Sail with me.   1120

PHILOCTETES

Are you crazy—me on the Trojan plains,
with the foul sons of Atreus, with this damned foot?

NEOPTOLEMUS
No. To men who'll heal your agonizing wound.

PHILOCTETES
A very cryptic statement. You mean . . .

NEOPTOLEMUS
I mean full flowering for you and me.

PHILOCTETES
Can you tell me that and not shake in shame
at the judgments of the gods?

NEOPTOLEMUS
Should a man who gives to his friend be ashamed?

PHILOCTETES
Gifts for me, or for Atreus' sons?

NEOPTOLEMUS
For you, my friend.   1130

PHILOCTETES
Oh yes, a real friend, who'll hand me over.

NEOPTOLEMUS
Don't let your misery turn you sour.

PHILOCTETES
I can tell your advice would destroy me.

NEOPTOLEMUS
You're the stubborn destroyer, not me.

PHILOCTETES
Did the Atridae maroon me? Did they?

NEOPTOLEMUS
>   They did. But now they'll save you.

PHILOCTETES
>   Not if I can help it. Not Troy.

NEOPTOLEMUS
>   What can I do? I can't convince you.
>   I should stop talking and leave you here,
>   marooned, absolutely hopeless.   1140

PHILOCTETES
>   My way's my way. But we joined hands
>   in an understanding: take me home, my son.
>   No more mention of Troy. I can't take any more.

NEOPTOLEMUS
>   All right. Let's go.

PHILOCTETES
>   Thank you for that. Let's go, then.

NEOPTOLEMUS
>   Can you walk well enough?

PHILOCTETES
>   I'll try as hard as I can.

NEOPTOLEMUS
>   But the rage of the Greeks will follow me.

PHILOCTETES
>   Ignore it.

NEOPTOLEMUS
>   And if they penetrate my boundaries?   1150

PHILOCTETES
    I'll be there.

NEOPTOLEMUS
    What good will that do?

PHILOCTETES
    The good of the bow.

NEOPTOLEMUS
    And you'll . . .

PHILOCTETES
    I'll make them run.

NEOPTOLEMUS
    Kiss the earth. It's goodbye. Let's go.
    (Heracles appears on the rocks behind the cave.)

HERACLES
    Stay, son of Poeas,
    until you've heard me.
    Heracles stands in front of you.
    The voice of Heracles sounds in your ears.   1160
    I've come from Olympus because of you.
    Through me great Zeus
    turns you back from your way.
    Listen.

    First my story, of intense endurance and pain,
    of a final arrival, to final recognition
    beyond death. Your life,
    like mine, will come through pain
    to such heightenings.
    Go to Troy with this man   1170
    to be healed, to be first for your power

and with my bow to topple Paris,
seed of all the suffering.
You will waste Troy, your peers
will honor you, you will bear the spoils
to your father Poeas and your country Oeta.
And remember, as tribute to my bow,
some part of those spoils on my pyre.

And you, son of Achilles, you cannot take
the city alone, nor he without you.   1180
You shall guard each other
like two lions on the hunt.
I will send the healer Asclepius to Troy
to return your health; my arms
will crack Troy twice.
But remember—when you burn the city,
honor the gods, for Zeus the highest virtue.
The sacred survives the graves.

PHILOCTETES
I've longed so long for your voice,
your form returning after such losses.   1190
I will not disobey you.

NEOPTOLEMUS
Neither will I.

HERACLES
Then get ready. The time is right
and the breeze able.
(Heracles goes.)

PHILOCTETES
So it's goodbye to you, companion cave,
nymphs of river and shore, beach-hollows
echoing ocean's deep music.

Sometimes the south wind brought me
the water's spray and wet my hair, myself
back by my cave's far wall, and I thought   1200
Mount Hermeaum answered my cries in kind.
Goodbye, Lycian well, I'm leaving you. I'd thought
Lemnos perpetual.
O my island, listen to me, sea-
surrounded host, your guest is going, wish him well
to his new harbor, appointed
by the powers of Fate and the great
voice whose will orders our event.

CHORUS

Let us pray to the sea nymphs
for bountiful winds and safe return.   1210
And then we can go.

Glossary

Achaea (a-kye'-a). Region in the northeast Peloponnese.

Achelous (a-kel'-oh-us). God of the river of the same name in Epirus.

Acheron (ak'-er-on). River in Epirus which, because of its dead appearance, was said to be one of the rivers of hell.

Achilles (a-kil'-eez). Son of Peleus and Thetis, the best of the Greek warriors at Troy, and hero of the *Iliad*.

Aegean Sea. Part of the Mediterranean between Greece and Asia Minor.

Aegisthus (ee-gis'-thus). Son of Thyestes, therefore a cousin of Agamemnon and Menelaus. Clytemnestra's lover.

Aenia (een'-i-a). City in Macedonia.

Aetolia (ee-tol'-i-a). Country in the middle of Greece of which Tydeus was king.

Agamemnon (ag-a-mem'-non). King of Mycenae, husband of Clytemnestra, and brother of Menelaus, king of Sparta. They were sons of Pleisthenes the son of Atreus (or, in some versions, they were themselves sons of Atreus).

Ajax (ay'-jaks). Son of Telamon king of Salamis and Eriboea, brother of Teucer. One of the great warriors at Troy.

Alcmene (alk-mee'-nee). Daughter of Electryon, mother of Heracles by Zeus, who appeared in her husband Amphitryon's shape.

Amphiaraus (am-fee-ar'-ee-us). One of the Seven against Thebes. Husband of Eriphyle, Adrastus' sister, father of Alcmaeon. Polynices bribed her with Harmonia's necklace to persuade Amphiaraus to participate in the war. Alcmaeon killed Eriphyle in revenge.

Antigone (an-ti'-go-nee). Daughter of Oedipus and Jocasta, sister of Eteocles, Polynices, and Ismene.

Antilochus (an-til'-o-kus). King of Messenia, son of Nestor.

Aphrodite (af-ro-dye'-tee). Latin Venus. Goddess of love.

Apollo (a-pol'-oh). God of music, healing, and prophecy. Son of Zeus and
   Leto, twin brother of Artemis.

Ares (air'-ez). Latin Mars. God of war.

Argos (ar'-gos). (1) Strictly speaking, an ancient city, the capital of Argolis
   in the Peloponnese. But all the inhabitants of the Peloponnese, and
   even all the Greeks, are called Argives. (2) Son of Zeus for whom
   the city was named.

Artemis (ar'-te-mis). Virgin goddess of the rural landscape and of hunting,
   prophecy, and childbirth. Daughter of Zeus and Leto, elder twin
   sister of Apollo.

Asclepius (es-klee'-pi-us). Son of Apollo, god of healing.

Asclepiadae (es-klee'-pi-a-dye). Followers of Asclepius, which is to say,
   doctors.

Athena (a-thee'-na). Latin Minerva. Goddess of wisdom and patroness of
   Athens.

Atreus (ay'-tree-us). Son of Pelops, father of Agamemnon and Menelaus,
   brother of Thyestes, whom he caused to eat the flesh of his own
   sons. (Or in some versions, he was the father of Pleisthenes and
   grandfather of Agamemnon and Menelaus.)

Atridae (a-trye'-dee). Agamemnon and Menelaus, the sons of Atreus, are
   often referred to as the Atridae; when this happens, the Greek uses
   "dual" forms for the verbs.

Aulis (owl'-is). Port in Boeotia where the Greek fleet gathered. The site of
   the sacrifice of Iphigenia.

Bacchus (bak'-us). God of wine and drinking, son of Zeus and Semele. The
   Bacchanalia were his festivals.

Barca (bar'-ka). Town in Lydia.

Boeotia (bee-oh'-sha). District in eastern Greece.

Cadmus (kad'-mus). Son of Agenor and brother of Europa. He established
   the country called Boeotia and founded the city of Thebes, which
   he populated with men (Spartoi) who sprang from the teeth of a
   dragon he had killed. He married Harmonia, and introduced the
   alphabet into Greece.

Calchas, or sometimes Kalchas (kal'-kus). Soothsayer who accompanied
   the Greeks, and who told Agamemnon at Aulis that he must sacrifice his daughter Iphigenia.

Cenaeum (se-nay'-um). A cape at Euboea.

Centaurs (sen'-taurz). Creatures who were half human and half horse; lived in Thessaly.

Cephallenia (sef-a-leen'-ya). An Ionian island.

Chiron (kye'-ron). Centaur who was wounded in the knee by a poisoned arrow of Heracles. The pain was so excruciating that he begged Zeus to deprive him of his immortality so he could die. He was placed among the constellations and became Sagittarius.

Chryse (kree'-say). Nymph who fell in love with Philoctetes and, when he rejected her, set a viper to bite him on the foot.

Chrysothemis (kri-so'-the-mis). One of the daughters of Agamemnon and Clytemnestra, sister of Orestes and Electra, and Iphigenia.

Clytemnestra (kly-tem-nes'-tra). Daughter of Leda, sister of Helen, wife of Agamemnon, mistress of Aegisthus, and mother of Iphigenia, Orestes, and Electra.

Colonus (ka-loh'-nas). Area in Attica north of the Acropolis.

Crete (kreet). Large Mediterranean island.

Crisa (kris'-a). Plain between Delphi and Corinth, sacred to Apollo.

Cronus (kro'-nus). Latin Saturn.Titan, son of Heaven (Uranus) and Earth (Gaia). He married his sister Rhea; their children included Demeter, Hades, Hera, Hestia, Poseidon, and Zeus, who overthrew him.

Cyprus (sye'-prus). Large Mediterranean island, birthplace of Aphrodite.

Deianira (day-a-nye'-ra). Daughter of Oeneus and Althaea, sister of Meleager, wife of Heracles.

Delos (del'-os). Small island, birthplace of Apollow and Artemis.

Delphi (del'-fye). Town on the southwest side of Mount Parnassus where the Pythia gave oracular messages inspired by Apollo.

Dionysus (di-o-nee'-sus). Another name for Bacchus. The Dionysia was the wine festival in the god's honor.

Dodona (do-doh'-na). Town in Epirus (some say Thessaly) where there was a temple to Zeus and the most ancient oracle of Greece. There was a grove of sacred oak trees surrounding the temple.

Echidna (ek-id'-na). Monster the upper part of whose body is that of a beautiful woman and the lower part that of a serpent.

Electra (e-lek'-tra). Daughter of Agamemnon and Clytemnestra, sister of Orestes, Iphigenia, and Chrysothemis.

Eriboea (er-i-bee'-a). Wife of Telamon and the mother of Ajax.

Erinyes (er-in′-yees). The Furies, the spirits of divine vengeance, who later become the Eumenides.

Erymanthus (er-i-man′-thus). Arcadian mountan, also a river and a town.

Euboea (you-bee′-a). The long island that stretches from the Gulf of Pagasae to Andros, the chief cities of which were Chalcis and Eretria.

Eurysaces (you-ris-ak′-eez). Son of Ajax and Tecmessa.

Eurystheus (you-ris′-thee-us). Son of Sthenelus and Nicippe, whose birth Hera hastens so that Heracles will have to be his servant. He was the one who ordered Heracles to perform his famous twelve labors.

Eurytus (you′-ri-tus). King of Oechalia, father of Iole.

Evenus (ev-ee′-nus). Son of Ares, father of Marpessa, whose virginity he protected by requiring her suitors to compete with him in chariot races. When Idas eloped with Marpessa, Evenus gave chase, but could not overtake the fleeing pair. He killed his horses and drowned himself in the Lycormas river, which was thereafter known as the Evenus.

Furies. See Erinyes.

Hades (hay′-deez). Latin Pluto. The world of the dead, or the god who ruled it.

Hector. Son of Priam and Hecuba, and the chief warrior of Troy. He married Andromache.

Helen. Daughter of Leda, sister of Clytemnestra, wife of Menelaus, taken by Paris to Troy.

Helenus (hel′-en-us). Son of Priam and Hecuba, a soothsayer. He married Andromache, widow of his brother Hector.

Hephaestus (hef-fes′-tus). Latin Vulcan. God of fire and smithing.

Hera (her′-a). Latin Juno. Wife and sister of Zeus, and queen of heaven.

Heracles (her′-a-kleez). Latin Hercules. Son of Zeus by Alcmene, husband of Deianira. He was tormented by Hera and made to perform many arduous labors.

Hermeaum (her-may′-um). Town of Arcadia.

Hermes (her′-meez). Latin Mercury. Son of Zeus and Maia. He was the messenger god and patron of messengers and merchants.

Hippodamia (hip-o-dam′-i-a). Daughter of Oenomaus of Pisa, who refused to let her marry unless her suitor could defeat him in a chariot

race. Those who lost had to forfeit their lives. Thirteen such suitors
had perished when Pelops appeared, bribed Myrtilius, Oenomaus.
charioteer, and thus contrived to win her.

Hydra. Monster that lived in lake Lerna in the Peloponnese. It had a hundred heads, and as soon as one was cut off, two more grew from
the wound. Heracles nonetheless killed it.

Hyllus (hill'-us). Son of Heracles and Deianira.

Ilium (il'-i-um) or Ilion. Name for Troy.

Io (eye'-oh). Daughter of the river Inachus, raped and turned into a white
cow by Zeus. Tormented by a gadfly sent by Hera, she wandered
all over the world until Zeus restored her.

Iole (eye'-o-lay). Daughter of Eurytus, captive of Heracles.

Iphianassa (if-i-a-nas'-sa). Daughter of Agamemnon and Clytemnestra, sister of Electra.

Iphigenia (if-i-jin-eye'-a). Daughter of Agamemnon and Clytemnestra
whom he sacrificed at Aulis.

Iphitus (if'-it-tus), Son of Eurytus whom Heracles kills.

Ithaca. Island off the western coast of Greece of which Odysseus was king.

Itys (it'-is). Son of Tereus, king of Thrace, and Procne, who was killed by
his mother and served up as meat for his father. He was changed
into a pheasant, his mother into a nightingale, and his father into
an owl or hoopoe.

Laertes (lay-air'-tees). Father of Odysseus.

Laomedon (lay-ah'-me-don). King of Troy, father of Priam.

Lemnos (lem'-nos). Island in the Aegean sacred to Hephaestus, now called
Stalimine.

Lerna. Lake where the Hydra lived.

Libya. Pretty much all of Africa except for Egypt.

Lichas (lik'-as). Herald of Heracles

Locris (lok'-ris). Region of Greece north of the bay of Corinth.

Lycia (li'-si-a). Country of Asia Minor.

Lycomedes (ly-kom'-e-deez). King of Scyros, the island on which Achilles
hid among the women to avoid service in the Trojan war. His
daughter, Deidamia, married Achilles and bore Neoptolemus.

Lydia (li'-di-a). Kingdom of Asia Minor; Croesus was its king.

Magnesia. Town of Asia Minor on the Meander river, a few miles from Ephesus.

Maia (mye'-a). Daughter of Atlas and one of the Pleiades, mother of Hermes by Zeus.

Malis (ma'-lis). One of Omphale's women servants whom Heracles loves.

Menelaus (me-ne-lay'-us). King of Sparta, son of Atreus, brother of Agamemnon, husband of Helen.

Mycenae (my-see'-nee). Town in the Peloponnese where Agamemnon ruled.

Myrtilus (mir-til'-us). Charioteer to Oenomaus (q.v.).

Mysia (miz'-i-a). Country of Asia Minor adjoining Phrygia.

Nemea (nem'-i-a). Town of Argolis near the wood where Heracles killed the lion.

Nemesis (nem'-e-sis). Goddess of divine vengeance, daughter of Oceanus.

Neoptolemus (ne-op-tol'-e-mus). Son of Achilles and Deidamia, also called Pyrrhus (yellow) because of the color of his hair.

Nessus (nes'-us). Centaur who tried to rape Deianira. Heracles shot him with a poisoned arrow. Nessus as he died gave his blood to Deianira, telling her it would restore a lover's interest. Actually, it was deadly poison and, when Deianira used it, it killed Heracles.

Nestor (nes'-tor). Son of Neleus and Chloris, companion of Menelaus.

Niobe (ny'-o-bee). Daughter of Tantalus, wife of Amphion of Thebes. She boasted that she was superior to Leto because of her many children, whereupon Leto's children Apollo and Artemis killed Niobe's children. She returned to Lydia, her native land, and was transformed to stone from which tears flowed continually.

Odysseus (o-dis'-yus). Latin Ulysses. King of Ithaca and one of the Greek heroes of the Trojan war. His domestic situation with faithful Penelope awaiting his return is often contrasted with Agamemnon's difficulties.

Oechalia (ee-kal'-i-a). Region and town in the Peloponnese of which Eurytus was king. It was destroyed by Heracles.

Oenomaus (ee-no-mah'-us). King of Pisa (the area around Olympia), father of Hippodamia, whom he promised to whoever could defeat him in a chariot race. Pelops did so by trickery.

Oeta (eet'-a). Mountain between Thessaly and Macedonia on which Heracles died.

Omphale (om-fal'-ay). Queen of Lydia to whom Hermes sold Heracles as a slave.

Orestes (or-es'-teez). Son of Agamemnon and Clytemnestra, brother of Electra, Iphigenia, and Chrysothemis. Married Hermione.

Ortygia (or-tij'-a). Ancient name for Delos, birthplace of Artemis and Apollo.

Pactolus (pak'-to-lus). Lydian river rising on Mount Tmolus.

Pallas (pal'-us). Name for Athena.

Pan. God of shepherds and hunters. He had horns and goat feet and invented the syrinx or reed flute.

Paris. Son of Priam and Hecuba who abducted Helen from Sparta.

Patroclus (pat-rok'-lus). A Greek warrior who was Achilles' close friend.

Pelops (pel'-ops). Son of Tantalus, who cut him up and served him to the Phrygian gods. Restored to life, he obtained Hippodamia after defeating Oenomaus in a chariot race by trickery. Father of Atreus.

Peparethos (pep-ar-eth'-us). Island in the Aegean off the Macedonian coast.

Persephone (per-sef'-o-nee). Latin Proserpine. Daughter of Demeter and queen of Hades.

Phanoteus (fan-oh'-te-us). Uncle of Strophius who was said to have fought with his brother Crisus in the womb. Crisus was Strophius' father and Pylades' grandfather. Orestes claims to be Phanoteus' messenger.

Philoctetes (fil-ok-tee'-teez). Son of Poeas and Demonassa, one of the Argonauts, who is was put ashore on the island of Chryse because of the foul smelling wound to his foot.

Phocis (foh'-kis). District of Greece next to Boeotia on the Gulf of Corinth.

Phoebus (fee'-bus). Name for Apollo.

Phoenix (fee'-nix). Son of Amyntor, king of Argos, who was tutor to Achilles and foster father of Achilles' son Neoptolemus.

Phrygia (fri'-jee-a). Country in Asia Minor.

Pleuron (plow'-ron). Land where Oeneus ruled and from which his daughter Deianira came.

Poeas (pee'-as). Father of Philoctetes.

Poseidon (po-sye'-don). Latin Neptune. God of the sea, brother of Demeter, Hades, Hera, Hestia, and Zeus.

Procne (prok'-ne). Daughter of Pandion, sister of Philomela. Her husband
	Tereus raped Philomela and cut out her tongue to guarantee her
	silence, but she wove the story into a piece of cloth and sent it to
	Procne. In revenge, Procne killed her son Itys and served him to
	Tereus.

Priam (prye'-am). King of Troy, son of Laomedon.

Pylades (pye'-la-deez). Son of Strophius, companion and cousin of Orestes.

Pythia (pith'-ee-a). The oracle of Apollo at Delphi, which was the site of the
	Pythian games.

Salamis (sal'-a-mis). Island in the Saronic Gulf off Eleusis, home of Ajax
	and Teucer.

Scamander (ska-man'-der). River near Troy.

Scyros (skee'-ros). Island off Euboea.

Sigeum (si-gay'-um). A town of the Troad on the promontory of the same
	name where the Scamander meets the sea.

Sisyphus (si'-si-fus). Son of Aeolus, king of Corinth. Tried to cheat Death,
	condemned in Hades endlessly to roll a huge stone up a mountain.

Spercheus (sper'-kee-os). River of Thessaly arising on mount Oeta.

Strophius (stro'-fee-us). King of Phocis, brother-in-law of Agamemnon,
	and father of Pylades.

Tantalus (tan'-ta-lus). King of Phrygia, son of Zeus, father of Pelops and
	Niobe.

Tecmessa (tek-mess'-a). Daughter of Teleutas, killed by Ajax, whose prop-
	erty she became and to whom she bore Eurysaces.

Telamon (tel'-a-mon). King of Salamis, comrade of Heracles, father of Ajax
	and Teucer.

Teleutas (tel-oo'-tas). Father of Tecmessa.

Teucer (too'-ser). Son of Telamon king of Salamis, by Hesione.

Thebes (theebz). City in Boeotia.

Themis (them'-is). Daughter of Uranus and Gaia who married Zeus and
	was the mother of the Horae (the Hours)—Diké (justice), Eirene
	(peace), Eunomia (good order)—and the Moirae (the Fates).

Thermopylae (ther-mop'-i-lee). Literally, the hot gates, the narrow pass that
	leads from Thessaly into Locris and Phocis. It is best known for
	the battle fought there in 480 B.C. between the Greeks and the
	Persians.

Thersites (ther′-si-teez). Foul-mouthed Greek warrior whom Achilles killed.

Theseus (thee′-see-us). Son of Aegeus and Aethra and king of Athens.

Thessaly. Territory to the north of Greece proper.

Tiryns (tear′-inz). Town in the Peloponnese founded by Tiryns, son of Argos. It was Heracles' home.

Trachis (tray′-kis). Town on the bay of Malea, near mount Oeta.

Tydeus (tid′-ee-us). One of the Seven against Thebes, father of Diomedes.

Zeus (zoos). Latin Jupiter. Son of the Titans Cronus and Rhea, brother of Demeter, Hades, Hera (whom he married), Hestia, and Poseidon. After he overthrew Cronus he became the chief Greek god.

About the Translators

BRENDAN GALVIN is the author of a dozen volumes of poetry, including *Great Blue: New and Selected Poems, Sky and Island Light*, and *Hotel Malabar*. He has been awarded fellowships from the Guggenheim Foundation and the National Endowment for the Arts, as well as the Iowa Poetry Prize, the Southeby Prize, *Poetry*'s Levinson Prize, the first O. B. Hardison, Jr. Poetry Prize of the Folger Shakespeare Library, and the International Poetry Forum's Charity Randall Citation. He received his Ph.D. degree from the University of Massachusetts and, since 1963, he has taught English and creative writing at several colleges in the Northeast, In 1993 he was the Coal Royalty Visiting Chairholder in Creative Writing at the University of Alabama. He lives in Truro, Massachusetts.

KENNETH MCLEISH was born in Yorkshire, England, and educated at Bradford Grammar School and Worcester College, Oxford, where he was a Senior Scholar in Classics. He was a schoolmaster before he became a fulltime writer. Over sixty of his translations have been performed on stage, television, and radio. He translated plays by Euripides, Sophocles, Feydeau, Horváth, Ibsen, Jarry, Labiche, Molière, and Strindberg. Among his many books are *The Theatre of Aristophanes, Shakespeare's People*, and *The Penguin Companion to the Arts in the Twentieth Century*, as well as guides to music and reading. He was also a composer whose works have aired on the BBC's Radio 3. A Fellow of the Royal Society of Literature, he lived in Lincolnshire, England. He died as this book was going to press.

FREDERIC RAPHAEL was born in Chicago and was educated at Charterhouse School and St. John's College, Cambridge, where he was awarded the Harper Wood Studentship. His first novel was published in 1956, and he has subsequently published twenty novels, four volumes of short stories, two biographies, and two volumes of essays, one of which, *Of*

Gods and Men, contains recensions of Greek myths. He has written (and occasionally directed) a number of screenplays for film and television, as well as five radio plays, several of them on classical themes. He received the 1996 American Academy Award for *Darling*, and has received many other awards for his screenplays. The television series *The Glittering Prizes* gained him the Writer of the Year award from the Royal Television Society. His translations, in collaboration with Kenneth McLeish, include the complete plays of Aeschylus (broadcast in 1978 on BBC television and in 1995 on the BBC world service), and Euripides' *Medea* and *The Bacchae*. He is a Fellow of the Royal Society of Literature. He divides his time between England and France.

A R M A N D   S C H W E R N E R   has published fifteen volumes of poetry, and his work has been included in over fifty anthologies. His poetry has been translated into French, German, Italian, Flemish, and Serbo-Croatian, it has also has been performed by himself throughout the world and adapted by dramatists, dancer-choreographers, and opera composers. Deeply indebted to Schwerner's studies of Buddhism and anthropology, his original poetry is an unusual amalgamation of ritual texts and postmodern experimentation. He is professor emeritus at the College of Staten Island of the City University of New York.

H E N R Y   T A Y L O R ,   a graduate of the University of Virginia, is Professor of Literature and Codirector of the MFA program in creative writing at the American University. He has received grants from the National Endowment for the Arts and the National Endowment of the Humanities, and has been awarded the Witter Bynner Prize for Poetry of the American Academy and Institute of Arts and Letters. He has published four volumes of original poetry, including *The Horse Show at Midnight*, *Breakings*, and, most recently, *Understanding Fiction*. In 1986 he received the Pulitzer Prize for his third collection of poetry, *The Flying Change*.